D0908522

C8

A Troubled Grandeur

A Troubled Grandeur

The Story of England's Great Actress, Sarah Siddons

by Marian Jonson

Little, Brown and Company — Boston — Toronto

LIBRARY OF CONGRESS CATALOG CARD NO. 72–182250

FIRST EDITION

T10/72

The author is grateful to Hawthorn Books Inc. for permission to
quote from *The Dramatic Imagination*, copyright 1941 by Robert
Edmond Jones.

Published simultaneously in Canada
by Little, Brown & Company (Canada) Limited

PRINTED IN THE UNITED STATES OF AMERICA

To Jerry and Joe

Acknowledgments

MY THANKS to the many people who kindly offered help in locating material for this book, in particular to the following:

Mr. Peter Delaney of Clackamas Community College for his suggestions on background reading and the generous amount of time he gave to discussions of the period.

Mr. John G. F. Miller of London for his help in finding maps, calendars, and other information.

Mrs. Ronald S. Callvert, of the research staff of *Gourmet* magazine, for her assistance in locating material on foods, wines, and taverns of the period.

Dr. Jeffrey Kindley of Columbia University for his help in locating material on the fires and riots of London theatres.

Mrs. Luceil Osvold for material and information concerning Bath.

Miss Peg Litherbury, children's librarian of the Port-

Acknowledgments

land Library Association, for her many helpful suggestions and encouragement.

Dr. Joseph F. Paquet of Portland for his helpful information concerning medical practice of the period.

Dr. Ronald Drennan of Portland for information on dentistry of the eighteenth century.

Miss Louise Sinnard for help in locating books and material.

Mrs. Peter L. Hurst of Portland for making available to me one of Mrs. Siddons' letters.

The quotation from *The Dramatic Imagination* by Robert Edmond Jones, copyright 1941 by Robert Edmond Jones, is reprinted with the permission of Hawthorn Books, Inc.

Author's Note

A BIOGRAPHER becomes a detective, searching for clues, sifting and balancing the evidence of letters, play reviews, diaries and reminiscences, pouncing with excitement on a date, a sentence in an old letter that may give an answer to the questions: What really happened at this moment or that? Under the trappings of theatre fame, who was the real Sarah Siddons? What did she feel and think? When the evidence conflicts, what is the truth that lies hidden somewhere in the tangle of clues?

The scholarly biographer, writing for other scholars, may lay the evidence out in bits upon the page, saying, "It is probable that . . ." or "It would seem that Sarah may have . . ." But the biographer writing for those interested more in the person than in scholarly puzzles must make decisions, must, like the detective, dare to say, "Aha! So that must be the answer!" And once the answer is decided upon, the biographer then tries to bring new life to the people and events of long ago.

In doing this, I have sometimes used the material from letters and other papers in conversational scenes.

For example, in the beginning of Chapter 8, where Sarah and William stand on the deck of the ship, I have had Sarah say to William the words she actually used in a letter sometime later about the embarkation for Ireland. In the scene with Richard Brinsley Sheridan in Chapter 7, I have put into dialogue the commitment to the problems of his time so evident in Sheridan's Parliamentary speeches and work. At times, in conversational scenes, I have made up a few sentences or simplified the elegant formalities of eighteenth-century speech, though the scenes are based on historical documentation. The majority of the time, I have used Sarah's own words. Where, as in the puzzle of Sarah's relationship to David Garrick, her own reminiscences as an old lady seem to differ from the evidence at the time of the events, I have relied more on the latter.

In all cases, my effort has been to remain faithful to the truth of the characters but to bring that truth into active scenes happening before us. As Sarah Siddons studied the words in a printed playscript and then made them into a living character onstage, so I have tried to bring the character of Sarah herself alive. This book, then, is perhaps less a narrative than a dramatized biography.

Marian Jonson

Portland, Oregon

Contents

xi

Prologue

Here is the secret of the flame that burns in the work of the great artists of the theatre. They seem so much more aware than we are, and so much more awake, and so much more alive that they make us feel that what we call living is not living at all, but a kind of sleep. Their knowledge, their wealth of emotion, their wonder, their elation, their swift clear seeing surrounds every occasion with a crowd of values that enriches it beyond anything which we, in our happy satisfaction, had ever imagined. In their hands it becomes not only a thing of beauty but a thing of power.

> — Robert Edmond Jones,
> *The Dramatic Imagination*

"None knew the troubled grandeur of guilt till they saw her in Lady Macbeth . . . more hideously troubled than ever was the hollow grave, seemed then, to be the cell of her heart."

> —John Wilson, Scottish critic

A Troubled Grandeur

Chapter One

"Just Learn Your Words, Luv"

"MY DAUGHTER SHALL NEVER MARRY AN ACTOR!" Roger Kemble shouted at young William Siddons, utility actor in his company. "You are dismissed, sir! On the instant!" Roger swept round to his weeping daughter. "As for you, Sarah, suitable employment will be found — not in the theatre!"

Sarah's howls of fury rose to match her father's shouts. The Kembles were a theatre family and their quarrels were not muted. The life Sarah had been planning as Mrs. Siddons, actress, now seemed forever ended. In fact, this moment of family uproar marked its real beginning.

Roger Kemble was himself an actor and the manager of a company of strolling players who toured the market towns of the English West Midlands. At thirty he had abandoned his secure trade as a barber and wig-maker to become an actor with John Ward's company. He had married Ward's daughter, Sarah, and eventually inherited his father-in-law's stock of battered scenery and costumes, the "goodwill" of his circuit, and the responsibilities of management. Renaming the troupe Mr. Kemble's Company of Comedians, Roger set out to build a reputation and found a family. In the latter he was highly successful, and he had determined that his children would have respectable homes and secure incomes. It had never occurred to him or Mrs. Kemble that any of their numerous brood might truly prefer the happy-go-lucky life of traveling actors. Now Roger looked with amazement at his eldest daughter as she declaimed between sobs that it was exactly the life she wanted.

Sarah glared back at her father, as baffled as he was. Why had her father changed so? He had always been the most genial and sympathetic of men. It was her mother who had disciplined the children. Now her father was shouting orders. Certainly it had begun peacefully enough, that summer of 1771, and everything had gone as usual — until July 5, her sixteenth birthday. From that evening, nothing had been quite the same. They were in Worcester that day, a market town on the Severn River, and getting ready for the evening's performance.

"Five minutes! Five minutes, ladies and gentlemen!" Roger boomed out the call and gave a final tug at his false beard. The players hurried through the last details of makeup, dusted fresh powder over their wigs, and began searching through the prop baskets for swords and fans and snuff boxes. It was five minutes to curtain in the Theatre at the King's Head, an ancient barn behind the King's Head Inn.

Sarah glanced again in the mirror, dabbed a spot of carmine at the inner corners of her eyelids. The quickening scene around her was familiar from childhood, but tonight it had a special excitement. The mirror reflected her slow, dark-eyed smile. Sixteen! No more school, no more child parts, no more walking under the drum in the Procession of Players. She was now a juvenile leading lady. Sixteen! Old enough to tell William Siddons she would marry him. Tonight was the beginning! She swept an extra measure of golden red powder over her pyramided curls.

All across England that hot July evening a similar ritual was being repeated. In barns and inn yards, tumbledown coach houses and tavern common rooms actors were making ready for the six o'clock performance. A rollicking, bawdy, gallant lot, they were never more than a leap ahead of the law that classed them as vagrants and placed them at the mercy of puritanical mayors, who could jail them, stone them from town, or bar them with signs proclaiming *No Gypsies, Monkeys or Actors!* Puritan influence was still strong in England, and many a magistrate believed that Sin and the Devil rode into town on the laughter of the players.

Sarah's mother now warbled a practice note or two. Mrs. Downing, the trollopy character actress, whooshed a final brush of powder over her husband's perpetually red nose. Fourteen-year-old John Philip Kemble yanked his sword belt fast and threw a punch at his younger brother Stephen's padded stomach. Their eleven-year-old sister, Frances, stood at the special-effects barrel, ready to beat the snuffer against a candlestick for the offstage sound of a windmill turning. Shouts from the audience greeted William Siddons as he stepped out to place the candles that would light the rickety platform stage. Her father, Sarah knew, was planning to start using floats — glass bowls of oil with multiple wicks burning in them — because they were safer, but William enjoyed the ceremony of lighting the candles. Blond and handsome, William was popular with audiences, if not with Roger Kemble.

Sarah stood ready in the dressing room. On ordinary nights it was the tackroom of the old barn, but now, draped with a bedraggled blanket to divide the men's from the women's space, it was labeled Dressing Room. To Sarah it was magnificent. Like all strolling players, she was accustomed to dressing in woodsheds, drafty inn hallways and tavern kitchens. Here at the King's Head, the company had a whole room just for dressing and makeup and still another room where they could stow their stage effects: the tall, rectangular, wood and paper "wings" painted to represent castle, garden, street and throne room scenes, and the hampers of swords, fans, crowns, daggers, devil's horns, trumpets and assorted oddments that made up their store of stage properties.

Boisterous shouts from the audience demanded that the play begin. As most country managers did, Roger Kemble evaded payment of a theatrical license by billing "A Concert of Music," and advertising that a play would be given free "between the parts of the Concert." If Mrs. Kemble or one of the children sang a few songs and played the guitar, the law was satisfied and the players safe from jail. The knowing townspeople bought tickets for the concert and came to see the play. In towns where the magistrates were especially touchy, even the concert was free, but Roger made it known that packets of toothpowder "fresh from London" were to be had for two shillings, one shilling, and sixpence. The toothpowder customers understood that for the two-shilling packets they could sit in "the boxes" — hastily swept-out horse stalls — but that for the cheaper packets they must shove themselves into whatever places they could find on the wooden benches.

Roger gave the signal for his actors to take their places. Quickly they touched good-luck pieces, spat, or crossed themselves. Sarah whispered something to William as he came backstage. He bent down and kissed her exuberantly. With a furious exclamation, Roger moved to separate them. It was too late. Raucous cheers were already greeting Mrs. Kemble as she stepped from the wings and began the song which was a Prologue to the play. Roger's cue came next. Glaring at William, he stepped to his place in the wings. The play had begun.

In the shadows offstage, Sarah moved to her own place. She felt a familiar surge of excitement, as if her body and mind were on tiptoe, waiting for the cue that would send her on. There! On she swept, made her brief curtsy to the audience, and began her evening's work. Though why anyone should call acting work was beyond her. It was so easy!

And such fun. Her parents had long ago taught her all there was to know about it. Throw your arms wide for joy, cock an eyebrow and flick your fan for coquetry, beat on your forehead and hurl yourself sobbing to the floor in despair — being careful, of course, to keep your hoops from flopping up in unexpected comedy. Her father thought she performed dying scenes admirably, launching herself into them with wild shrieks, then sinking gracefully into her last delicate gasps upon the floor, until she expired with a final imploring gesture that made gentry and shopkeepers weep to watch her.

Mrs. Kemble had been most particular about training her children in gesture and in voice and diction. "Brrr-eathe deee-ply!" she would say, inhaling vast quantities of air, "then speak your words dist-in-ct-ly!" No one ever mentioned characterization. All great ladies were elegant, all servingmaids and farm wives hearty and coarse. That was all there was to it.

Occasionally London actors down on their luck wandered into the Kemble company for a brief time. Invariably they would talk of the new natural acting. "Act from Nature!" they would insist. "That's as the great David Garrick does it." Roger Kemble only snorted. His advice to each of his children was the same: "Just learn your words, luv, and motion as your mother tells you." It would take years of experience — and scarring failure — before Sarah would understand why now, when she was sure she knew all about acting, she had scarcely begun to learn. The ranting bellow, the sing-song declamation, the wide-flung exaggerated gestures were already outmoded, but this was the style of acting small-town audiences still loved and expected.

Audiences expected, too, that each arriving troupe of actors, in the bright shabby splendor of costumes, swords and gilt paper crowns, would march through town in a grand Procession of Players. When the Kembles paraded in Worcester, John Philip led off as usual, beating the drum small Frances balanced on her head. Sarah came next with William, and her parents followed, Roger beaming and waving as Stephen and the younger children dashed ahead handing out playbills to the gawking housewives, farmers and local gentry.

Roger Kemble knew that a manager of honest character with an amiable wife and a goodly number of children appealed to the gentry of these provincial towns and deterred mayors from stopping the performances. In a burst of pride he raised his wife's hand with his own in a mutual salute to the gentlemen watching. Mrs. Kemble, Roger acknowledged, was indeed an amiable wife, if a trifle sharp-tongued when he'd had a glass too many. He peered over his shoulder to check on his character actors, the Downings. Yes, there was poor Downing puffing along, mopping his shining nose while Mrs. Downing leered at the fishmonger as she paraded past.

Sarah smiled tolerantly as motherly souls along the streets pointed at Frances and sputtered, "Wonder it won't addle the poor child's wits, having 'er head beat on like that!" and were often answered with a shrugged, "Actors! Mad folk, anyway." Sarah had walked under the drum as a child and knew it had given her a queenly carriage of head and shoulders. Now the fishmongers and country squires who watched the Procession loudly admired the tall, chestnut-haired girl who moved with such a lithe and easy grace, head high and shoulders straight.

Sarah had learned early, of course, that ordinary people scorned the strolling players. For players had no homes where they lived month in, month out; they were almost always poor; and sometimes when, as actors like Roger might say, dire misfortune had befallen, they would creep barefoot at midnight from an inn to avoid the bill, or filch apples and turnips from farms they trundled past. When money was scarce, they walked from town to town, pulling their carts piled with scenery and costumes and often with a baby snuggled among the hoops and velvets.

Now that the Kemble players were well established on their circuit, they traveled in ease. Women and girls were packed inside a creaking, high-wheeled coach, while the boys and men clung to the straps that held their luggage to the roof or clambered onto the wooden wagons following with their stage effects. Shouting at the horses, waving greetings and good-byes to the stolid-faced weavers and farmers they passed, the players jounced from town to town over the rutted country roads.

To Sarah and the younger Kembles, life on tour was a perpetual excitement, even when a muddy curve sent the coach slithering off the road. Then what a screeching and scrambling there would be! The women all shrieking and gasping over their smelling salts, the men picking themselves from the ditch and feeling for broken bones as the boys dashed to gather up costumes and props — King Charles' golden crown from a nearby bush or Mrs. Kemble's best hoop rolling erratically down the road. Sarah knew it was the judgment of ordinary people — actors are mad folk — but she hated the one taste she had had of ordinary life.

When she was twelve, the Kembles had spent several months in Worcester. Mrs. Harries, mistress of Thornloe House School, graciously recognizing the Kembles' comparative respectability, had given Sarah free tuition. The girls immediately made her feel their disdain, and Sarah made no effort to secure their friendship. She merely withdrew into the cool dignity that later would become characteristic of her whenever she felt shy or hurt. Sarah was aware the girls talked about her; she was unaware that one had written home:

> A new pupil has been added to our number, a Miss Sarah Kemble. . . . She is very plain in cloaths, and thought somewhat of a Brown Beauty, for her eyes and features, with the exception of a somewhat too long nose, merit much commendation. Her manner was not pleasing, withdrawing from our company, and holding herself aloof from our amusements.
>
> . . . I asked her what her parents were, and what their position, as indeed, dear Mama, you have advised me to do, to avoid the possibility of becoming intimate with an unsuitable or ungenteel acquaintance. But she answered without blush or confusion that her father was Roger Kemble, the manager of a troupe of Strolling Players, who had arrived in town travelling in a waggon.

You can imagine my embarrassment, my dear Mama, at having exhorted so damaging a confession . . .

When it was discovered that Sarah could make wonderful costumes from butcher's paper, the girls overcame their embarrassment. Sarah cared little if they did or not. She could sing and play the harpsichord, and *she could act*. What did school matter? She walked away from it delighted when the Kembles again took to the road, and went back to reading the books she loved, especially Milton's poetry and Shakespeare's plays.

Now, at sixteen, strolling was Sarah's chosen life. She could imagine no other. Yet she knew that after this summer it would be different. This was the last summer the Kembles would live their strolling life together. Her parents had other plans for their children. This fall, John Philip would go to Douai, France, to study for the priesthood, and in a year or two Stephen would join him. Frances would be apprenticed to a milliner and Elizabeth to a dressmaker. Sarah wanted nothing but to continue acting with her Sid.

Her father had tried to ignore the fact that William and Sarah now called each other Sid and Sally. He put down his suspicion that they had "an understanding." He told himself and Mrs. Kemble that Sarah was sure to marry one of the landowning young squires who flocked to admire her red-brown hair and well-formed bosom. But the backstage kiss in the Theatre at the King's Head upset him thoroughly.

Roger had hardly changed from his costume after the show before he was in furious conference with Mrs. Kemble:

they must dismiss William at once. Best wait, cautioned Mrs. Kemble. They must remember that their audiences liked William, and after all, they had no other utility actor. Roger fumbled for a letter he had received from a young fellow wanting a job — a Thomas Holcroft. But, warned Mrs. Kemble, was Holcroft not the one who sounded such a radical? Well, yes, admitted Roger, the fellow had said he'd attended the Dissenters' schools, but what of that? The important thing was to get William Siddons away from Sarah: he would dispatch a letter to this Holcroft at once. Meanwhile, they would say nothing of the matter except to discourage William however they could. Sixteen, agreed Mrs. Kemble, was much too young to marry.

The players moved on to Hereford, which to most of them meant only that the inn would have good beef. Players had their own ways of remembering places. The usual sights meant nothing; the important thing about a town was the mayor's temper, the theatre they played, or the local food. Worcester was special for the old barn theatre, and to Sarah, for the Worcester fat cakes she loved, puffy brown balls of sweet dough deep-fried in boiling lard and sometimes dusted with sugar. The cathedral town of Coventry meant spires against the sky and bells booming out over the countryside to welcome travelers.

Hereford was beef and lamb and fruit from nearby orchards. And it was the last town they played before crossing the border into the Marches of Wales. Sarah had been born in Brecon, Wales, at the Shoulder of Mutton Inn on July 5, 1775, when her grandfather Ward's company was playing there. She had been christened there at St. Mary's in her mother's Church of England faith, though Philip and the other boys were to be Roman Catholic like their father.

It was in Hereford where Tom Holcroft caught up with the Kemble players. One evening as the tired actors were finishing their spit-roasted beef and the crisp pudding that baked beneath it, the inn door opened to a thin, shaky young man. "Mr. Roger Kemble?" he asked. Roger waved a greeting and continued to munch his plum tart. "I'm Holcroft. I wrote you — about acting in your company."

Sarah felt William abruptly stiffen beside her. Her father rose. "Mmm, ah — yes, Thomas Holcroft, to be sure! Ah, have you eaten?"

"No, I've not eaten," said Holcroft. "I have no money."

Instantly the actors came alive, making a place at the long table, pushing the wooden boards of bread and cheese toward Holcroft, and the remains of the roast and the platter of tarts. Quarrel as they sometimes did over parts and salaries and costumes, they knew how it felt to be hungry. They responded with a warm gathering in of the pale new actor. Only William remained aloof.

"That means your father's giving me notice," he whispered to Sarah.

"Why?"

"He saw me kiss you. He knows I want to marry you. Your mother says you're too young and your father threatend to give my notice of dismissal."

"I shall run away with you — to Scotland!"

William stared at her with sudden caution and turned to listen as Holcroft told how he had chased from town to town after the Kemble players, had run out of money and arrived in Hereford nearly starved. At first he had been directed to the lodgings of Mr. Kemble, the local barber.

"Good God, man, didn't they give you food or at least a tankard of ale?" exploded Mr. Downing, now on his own fourth tankard.

"No," said Holcroft. "They wanted naught to do with any strolling actor. They told me to try here, this was a sheep drovers' inn and a low enough place to look for actors. Thank God, I found you."

By the time they reached Brecon, the Kemble players were thoroughly split on the matter of whether William Siddons should marry Sarah Kemble. It had been a dull season if a profitable one; the players welcomed a romance and took impassioned sides. Bets were placed, angry words bandied, and lordly silences maintained. Even the family divided. John Philip favored William; Stephen wished that Sarah would fall in love with the aloof, superior Mr. Holcroft.

In Brecon, the Kembles were soon approached by a Mr. Evans, newly become the Squire of Pennant and entranced by Sarah's singing of "A Robyn, Gentil Robyn." He had, said the Squire, an income of three hundred pounds a year and several hundred acres of land. He wanted to marry Sarah. Her delighted parents promptly forgot she was too young.

Roger made it clear to William that he was to quit the

company, and offered him a benefit — a performance from which William would get the greatest share of the evening's profits. William sulked. Sarah accepted the Squire's invitation to walk with him about his woodlands. The townspeople talked: *Sarah and William would use the benefit money to elope! No! Sarah was madly in love with the Squire! Not so, she was fearful of her mother who had locked her in her room!*

Roger went about glowering. Mrs. Kemble enthusiastically promoted the joys of a settled home and a regular income, and tried to engage her obstinate daughter in conversation about the duties of a country gentleman's wife. William began writing on bits of paper, and muttering to himself.

On the night of William's benefit, the house was packed. William was cheered by his supporters and hissed by the Squire's friends. Each of the men in question remained silent. The first of the plays ended successfully. The actors retired backstage to switch beards and costumes for the second play. Someone noticed William was missing. He was still onstage.

The company rushed to the wings in time to hear him addressing the audience: ". . . and I have written this poem to commemorate the occasion. It is called 'A Lover Discarded.' Mrs. Kemble grabbed Roger as he was making a leap for the stage. William cleared his throat. "You will, I am sure, understand that the Colin referred to in the verse is — ah — myself." To shouts from the house, William began:

"Just Learn Your Words, Luv"

Ye ladies of Brecon, whose hearts ever feel
For wrongs like this I'm about to reveal . . .

Backstage, Roger struggled to get loose as Mr. Downing and John Philip held him back. William continued, his gestures growing enthusiastic:

But soon she convinced him 'twas all a mere joke,
For duty rose up, and her vows were all broke.

Sarah shrieked a protest. "I did not break my vows!" Her words were lost in the hissing out front.

She acquainted her Ma, who, her ends to obtain,
Determined poor Colin to drive from the plain.

Mrs. Downing leaned excitedly toward the stage, spilling powder over Roger's head. William rose to the climax of his poem.

. . . accept the poor thanks of a lover discarded!

William bowed to the stamping, cheering house. Glowing with triumph he strode backstage and was bounced against the wall as Mrs. Kemble whacked him on one ear and then the other until Mrs. Downing and a screaming Sarah pulled her away.

"You are dismissed, sir!" Roger shouted. "Dismissed on the instant!"

"Fight him a duel, Pa!" yelled Stephen as Frances clapped her hand over his mouth.

Sarah burst into tears. "Oh, Sid! I never meant to marry the Squire!"

"My daughter shall never marry an actor!" roared Roger as Mrs. Kemble joined in with a resounding, "Never!"

Sarah shouted back, *"You* did!"

"That is why . . ."

"Madame!" Roger was looking at his wife with the eyes of a wounded spaniel.

Suddenly the whole shouting, furious company doubled over in laughter. It was true, smiled Sarah's mother. She had, indeed, married an actor and been very happy.

The Squire fled from the theatre, relieved to have escaped this tempestuous girl and these mad people.

At last Roger agreed that perhaps, and only perhaps, his daughter might on some future day become Mrs. Siddons. Meanwhile William must leave the Kemble players. As for Sarah, suitable employment would be found — not in the theatre.

A few weeks later Roger saw his daughter onto the stage-coach for Warwick, where she would be employed as maid-companion to the widowed Lady Mary Greatheed at Guy's Cliffe Manor.

Chapter Two

Guy's Cliffe and David Garrick

SARAH HAD BEEN AT GUY'S CLIFFE for more than a year when she met England's greatest actor, David Garrick. The meeting was unexpected, coming as it did in the midst of an ordinary morning.

Sarah had been curled on the window seat of her room where she could see the distant shimmer of the Avon River flowing past the groves of oak and pungent cedar. Nearby, the rich brown furrows of the garden were almost hidden under the spiky blades of onions and leeks, and the feathering tops of carrots. A tang of spice rose from the sun-warmed beds of thyme and parsley, rosemary, shallot and tarragon in the herb garden just below. How easy to become accustomed to all this: to the books and paintings, the silky fabrics and polished woods of this beautiful house. Sarah felt at peace here. To Guy's Cliffe and its sense of rest Sarah would return in times of trouble all her life.

She was almost eighteen now, clear-skinned and strong, her red-brown hair shining with the vigor country life had given her. It must be the food, she thought. Never had she eaten such food as here at Guy's Cliffe nor seen it so gracefully served. An endless stream of silver platters and delicate porcelain bowls heaped with savory abundance flowed from the bustling kitchens to the mahogany dining tables. Family and guests, house staff and farm workers ate the crusty wheaten loaves made from local grain, meat and chickens from the manor lands, and vegetables fresh from the garden. There were so many kinds of vegetables that Sarah had not yet learned the names of some of them, though she knew her favorite was the pale-green marrow sauced with sweet butter and chives. There was fruit of every sort from the orchard — plums and apples, peaches, nectarines and pears, dark red and purple berries — for tarts, puddings and glistening preserves. At Guy's Cliffe Sarah developed a love of good food that would last her lifetime.

In place of the stiff, hoop-skirted gowns of her stage costumes she now dressed in the simpler clothing of the serving staff. To feel her body moving free and lithe under the long, full, unwired skirts, to watch the folds of material follow and respond to her movement became an active physical joy.

Her duties were light. In the custom of the day Sarah had been accepted into the household "under the protection" of Lady Mary, who interpreted the phrase literally. With friendly protective warmth, she required little of Sarah beyond an occasional session of reading aloud while she worked at her embroidery or when the family gathered after dinner. When Lady Mary traveled to visit her father, the Duke of Ancaster, she took Sarah along as companion. So impressed was she by the tall girl's queenly bearing that she remarked later it was difficult to suppress the impulse to rise each time Sarah entered the room.

For the family Sarah often read Milton and Shakespeare, but she declaimed her more melodramatic scenes for the servants and Lady Mary's twelve-year-old son Bertie. The boy followed her about begging for the dying scenes she played with such gusto. Lady Mary's brother applauded Sarah's readings until the lady of the house chided him, "Brother, don't encourage the girl; you will make her go on the stage," and cautioned him that Mr. Kemble wanted his daughter to settle down. "Hmph! Pity!" muttered Lord Bertie and continued to applaud. Nonetheless Lady Mary secretly enjoyed the more vividly emotional interpretations of her companion and had to suppress her laughter at the unconscious imitations of her guests that sometimes crept into Sarah's acting.

Without knowing it Sarah was absorbing much from the people around her, the quality of sureness and ease they had, their speech and manners, the ways they handled themselves, their clothes and their silver at table. It gave her a knowledge no other actress of her time possessed. She alone had the dual experience of rough provincial strolling and aristocratic country living. During her years at Guy's Cliffe she

had time for books and walks, for letters and poems to her
Sid, who was allowed to visit her on the few occasions he had
money for travel. Then there were long strolls to the mill,
the wishing spring, or to Guy's Cave above the river. There
was talk of acting and marriage, but Sarah felt uncertain
now and turned away from any thought of leaving Guy's
Cliffe.

As she began giving more attention to the discussions she
heard — of ideas and books, of painting and music and
theatre — an idea grew. These people respected the ability
to do things well, whether it was growing healthy farm
crops or writing essays or acting in plays. To do things well
for the pure pleasure of excellence; it was a concept she had
never heard before. How well did she really act?

Was it true, she asked the servants, that the London actor
David Garrick visited sometimes at Guy's Cliffe? Oh, indeed, they assured her. Lady Mary and her brother thought
most highly of Mr. Garrick. Sarah wrote Garrick a letter
asking for an audition and "soliciting first his judgment,
and secondly, his protection." She addressed it to the Theatre Royal in Drury Lane, and sent it with the family post
to London. Nothing was heard from Mr. Garrick; Sarah
gave up hope that he would venture from London to see
her, and in the smoothness of life at Guy's Cliffe almost
forgot she had written.

Months later she was summoned one morning to the
drawing room. Lady Mary had guests and would like Sarah
to give a recitation for their enjoyment. As she entered the
room Sarah noted that these were unfamiliar guests, for-

eigners apparently. The woman's hair was gleaming black, piled high with a few artfully careless wisps curling down over her olive-skinned forehead. And her husband — French, perhaps, or Irish? He seemed neither young nor old — just vividly alive. In peacock silk breeches and coat he lounged at ease in his chair with a look of balance and alertness, as if he could spring up in one quick motion.

They smiled expectantly at Sarah. The man spoke first. "Hmm, well now — what will you give us, eh?"

"The Tragedy of Jane Shore, sir."

"The Shore, eh? Mmm, zounds!" One black eyebrow winged upward in amusement. "Ah — well then — let's have a roll and a tumble." A swift gesture of his hand, hardly raised from the chair arm, gave an unmistakable order to begin.

Annoyed, Sarah smoothed her skirt, then took a deep slow breath. "I shall play both Jane and Alicia," said Sarah, wishing to make everything quite clear to the guests. The man's amusement deepened. Sarah took another breath. Flinging her arms wide she addressed the heavens in Jane Shore's ringing tones:

> *Why should I wander . . .*
> *Stray further on, for I can die even here!*

With a long moan she wilted against a nearby table, then jerking upright, she leaped several steps to her left. "Now I am Alicia," she muttered, thrusting her hands through her hair until it was thoroughly scrambled. The playscript, she remembered, said, "Enter Alicia, in disorder." Sufficiently disordered, Sarah addressed the empty space where she had stood a moment before as the unfortunate Jane and demanded with a peremptory gesture:

> *What wretch are thou whose misery and baseness*
> *Hangs upon my door?*

She let the words roll out with all the resonant scorn of which she was capable, then could not resist a sidelong glance at the man watching her. He was not watching! Fingers over his lips as if to stifle a smile, he had risen and was moving toward the window, his back toward her. How dare he be so rude! She tried to hold down her temper. It was wrong, her father had taught her, for an actor to feel real anger when playing an angry scene, but . . . oh, what did it matter? This silk-clad dandy would never know if she acted well or ill.

Sarah continued, hurling the words toward the man's back, Alicia's words and Jane Shore's, but now filled with her own fury and hurt. She was hardly aware when he turned to face her, but his eyes were so darkly intent that she found herself addressing the last lines directly to him, unable to look away. Surprised, she heard herself changing the lines as country actors did to simpler ones. Quietly she spoke:

> *. . . have pity on me!*
> *You've never known the bitterness of want,*
> *And may you never know it.*

She waited. The man stared at her for a moment. His eyes suddenly sparkled. "Aha! Well, now! Comedy — Rosalind?"

Without waiting to arrange her dress Sarah launched into the Rosalind-Celia scene from Shakespeare's *As You Like It.* Laughing and teasing, shaking and slapping the air where the imagined Celia stood, Sarah sped through the lines, then dropped to her knees and concluded the scene with a flourish. She waited for the expected laughter. But the man's face was gentle, his eyes held a startled tenderness.

"Amazing!" Lady Mary's voice cut in. "Quite reminds one of Woffington in her youth." Lady Mary stopped, then quickly took another tack. "Thank you, Sarah. Quite delightful, wouldn't you say so, Mr. Garrick?"

Garrick! Sarah felt as if she might faint. To have cut loose like that and made a fool of herself before David Garrick! She forced herself steady, listening. . . .

". . . difficult, of course, for a very young woman. Ah, but then!" Garrick was smiling, giving her time to recover. "Best no introduction — see what you can really do — no fright before — eh?"

Sarah nodded, liking his odd way of speaking as if his mind darted ahead of his speech and must turn back and pick up the words in bits and pieces. Garrick began to discuss her work. He was pleased, he said, especially that in the Jane Shore she had somehow got rid of the usual country actors' singsong delivery, the provincial ti-tum-ti-tum rhythm of declamation. However, he could promise her no place at Drury Lane. He already had the well-known actresses Mrs. Yates, Mrs. Abington and Miss Younge for leading roles in addition to any number of bit players. As to the future, who could know?

Taking a sudden decision, Sarah answered, "In the future, sir, I shall be Mrs. Siddons."

Garrick rose and bowed. "I thank you for your audition. And now — good morning!"

Sarah was puzzled by Garrick's reaction to her audition. She had done the scenes all wrong, letting her own emotions overcome her knowledge of correct elocution. Yet he had liked it. Perhaps he was being kind? Very baffling, but perhaps not important.

She was fired now by dream and decision. Her life here at Guy's Cliffe had been the playing of a role — Maid-Companion to Lady Mary by Miss Kemble — and she must now move on to her own real life. She would marry William even if they had to elope to Scotland. She would return to the theatre. Together she and William would conquer London at the Theatre Royal in Drury Lane. The books and paintings, the good food and beautiful surroundings were not, as she had once thought, limited to those born to them. This way of life could be earned, as Garrick had earned it, by ability and work. She picked up her quill and wrote to William and her parents.

Sensing the new firmness in Sarah, the Kembles agreed to her marriage. The Greatheeds bade her a warm farewell; Lady Mary presented her with a leather-bound volume of Milton's poetry and young Bertie promised, "Someday I shall write a wonderful play for you to do in London!"

On the morning of November 26, 1773, the Kembles and William walked to Trinity Church in Coventry where Roger gave his eighteen-year-old daughter Sarah in marriage to William Siddons. Sarah and William at once rejoined the Kemble players. On December 13 Sarah made her first appearance on the playbill as MRS. SIDDONS. And Roger, observing his new son-in-law plodding through his part onstage, muttered, "I said my daughter would never marry an actor — *and she has not!*"

Sarah was soon pregnant but continued to work. William decided it was time to declare their independence and signed a contract with Chamberlain and Crump, whose disreputable management had earned them the nicknames of Fox and Bruin. Their company rarely played more than one night in a town. Life became a blur of passing villages and towns, of learn your words, mend your costumes, clamber into the coach, get to the next town, find the stage and somehow act. The dream of London seemed far away.

One night as the exhausted players entered the Black Bear Inn at Devizes, they encountered a small boy perched on the bar counter reciting Shakespeare. The innkeeper beamed as the actors applauded. "My son, Master Thomas Lawrence," he said. The boy scrambled down, ran for colored chalk and paper. Sketching quickly and with astonishing skill, he drew a picture of Sarah. She felt the tears rising; tired, dirty, heavily pregnant as she was, the boy had sketched her as he saw her, a young and beautiful actress. Impulsively she hugged him. "Thank you, Thomas Lawrence. Perhaps it will bring me good luck." She felt, somehow, that like sunshine the sketch would be a good omen.

Her first baby, a boy they christened Henry, was born on October 4, 1774. He was bundled along with the company and Sarah cradled him in costume hampers and nursed him backstage between acts.

At the holiday resort of Cheltenham, the company settled in for a longer stay and Sarah gained some rest. One evening a party of aristocratic ladies and gentlemen entered the theatre for Sarah's performance as Belvidera in *Venice Preserved*. It was a tragic role and as Sarah was pleading and storming her way through it she heard a strange muffled snorting. It came from the boxes occupied by the party. Sarah continued. The snorting and sniffling grew louder. She tensed — they were laughing at her! Sarah returned to her lodgings depressed and "grievously mortified."

The next morning William was stopped on the street by a gentleman who introduced himself as Lord Bruce, host of last evening's party. He wished to present his compliments to the lovely Mrs. Siddons. Unfortunately, the ladies of his party had been so moved by Mrs. Siddons' beautiful playing they were still confined to their rooms repairing the ravages of last night's tears. William, wrote Sarah later, "hastened home with all speed to comfort me with this intelligence."

That afternoon, Lord Bruce's step-daughter, Henrietta Boyle, called at the Siddonses' lodgings to pay her compliments. She was about Sarah's age, rich, beautiful, glowing with friendly common sense. Noting that the young actors were poor and guessing that they must provide their own costumes, Henrietta offered her help. She made costumes for

Sarah from her own stores of expensive materials, gave her jewelry, shawls, laces and gloves — all the accessories a young actress should have in her wardrobe but that Sarah could not afford. Henrietta's generosity was the sort of practical help Sarah needed if she were ever to rise beyond raggle-taggle companies like Crump's. And in the hours when Henrietta worked over the costumes, tactfully demonstrating how to wear them with style and flair, Sarah gained a lifelong friend.

When next in London, Lord Bruce approached David Garrick and gave him a glowing account of the young actress who was "a diamond in a dust-bin." Soon after, a trusted member of the Drury Lane company, Tom King, watched Mrs. Siddons in a performance of *The Fair Penitent* at Cheltenham. He reported enthusiastically to Garrick, noting that the actress had fine legs for the popular "breeches parts" in which a female character was clad in a young man's tight hose and silk breeches. But Garrick decided to wait.

Next year the Siddonses were again at Cheltenham but with a better company managed by Joseph Younger. Among the roles Younger assigned to Sarah was Lady Macbeth, a part she had not played before. As usual, Sarah began to study the role after Henry was tucked in bed and William began dozing in another room. The house was dark and quiet; there was no one near.

Sarah read through Lady Macbeth's first scene, in which she plans to murder the old king, Duncan, as he sleeps in her castle:

Guy's Cliffe and David Garrick

Come, thick night,
And pall thee in the dunnest smoke of hell,
That my keen knife see not the wound it makes.

The silence of the night seemed to thicken around her. She read on into the assassination scene where Lady Macbeth takes the bloody daggers from Macbeth and finds her own hands smeared with the murdered king's blood. She felt a sick knotting in her stomach; as she wrote later:

> . . . the horrors of the scene rose to a degree that made it impossible for me to get farther. I snatched up my candle, and hurried out of the room in a paroxysm of terror. My dress was of silk, and the rustling of it, as I ascended the stairs to go to bed, seemed to my panic-struck fancy like the movement of a spectre pursuing me. At last I reached my chamber, where I found my husband fast asleep. I clapt my candlestick down upon the table, without the power of putting the candle out, and I threw myself on the bed, without daring to stay even to take off my clothes.

The next morning Sarah rose early to resume work on the role but she was so shaken that her performance went badly.

Garrick now began making more detailed inquiries about Sarah. He appealed for help to his friend, the Reverend Henry Bate. Bate was known as a farmer, sportsman, and fighter, and more importantly as the owner of the London newspaper, the *Morning Post*. He was only incidentally a minister. He and his wife arrived in Cheltenham "after combatting the various difficulties of one of the cussedest crossroads in this kingdom" to scout Sarah's performance in *As You Like It.*

She was again pregnant and expecting her baby in late November. Mr. Bate, unable to get a seat for the show, watched from backstage in the tiny barn theatre and reported to Garrick:

> I beheld her from the side wings of the stage . . . I think she cannot fail to be a valuable acquisition to Drury Lane. Her figure must be remarkably fine, when she is happily delivered of a big belly. . . . Her face (if I could judge from where I saw it) is one of the most strikingly beautiful for stage effect that I ever beheld:

Mr. Bate heard gossip that scouts from Covent Garden, London's other Royal Patent theatre, were also in the area and interested in Sarah. Promptly he requested an interview with William, who as Sarah's husband managed all her contracts and, by the laws of the time, owned any money his wife earned. Bate informed Garrick that while William was "a damned rascally player" Sarah could not only act well but learn her lines rapidly. "She is the most extraordinary quick study I ever heard of. This cannot be amiss, for, if I recollect right, we have sufficient number of the leadenheaded ones at D. Lane already."

Garrick replied immediately that Bate was to inform Sarah that "she may depend on every reasonable and friendly encouragement in my power" and that if she "will be wholly governed by me, I will make her theatrical fortune." Unlike most theatre managers of his time Garrick directed his productions with great care and demanded much of his company. He taught them carefully and, said his famous actress, Kitty Clive, "with lamb-like patience." He wanted no actresses who were unwilling to accept his exacting and brilliant direction.

Garrick was somewhat disturbed by the news of Sarah's pregnancy. He had hoped to introduce her in October but he wrote Bate: "Your account of the *big belly* alarms me! — when shall we be in shapes again? how long does the lady count? when will she be ready to appear?" and asked him to have Sarah send a list of her favorite roles.

Letters flew back and forth, completing arrangements. Sarah would be "ready for service" in late December. Garrick gave the Siddonses money to live on while they awaited the baby and wrote William: "I beg that she will not make herself uneasy about coming, till she will run no risk of the journey." He wished William "joy of Mrs. Siddons' safe delivery, & I hope she continues well —"

On November 4 as Sarah was performing in Gloucester, she felt a shock of pain. Gasping, she recovered and continued her lines. Again it came. The baby was not due for three more weeks! She struggled through the remaining scenes of the play. Early the next morning her baby was born, a girl christened Sarah Martha, and never called anything but Sally.

A month later Sarah, William, and their two babies set out for London. After five days in an unheated stagecoach, joggling along muddy, slippery roads and stopping by night at roadside inns, they entered the jammed and noisy streets of London. On December 29, 1775, Sarah was to make her first appearance at the Theatre Royal in Drury Lane. The dream was true — and she was twenty.

Chapter Three

Dream into Nightmare

LONDON! To Sarah it was an incredible fantasy of beauty and filth. Spacious and parklike, crowded and noisy, smelling of sea salt and tarred ropes, coffee and spices and acrid-burning coal, London held all the excitement of the future. And the future began now.

She could scarcely wait for the first day of rehearsal, yet she wanted to see everything in the city. There were tree-lined parks that opened out over the River Thames and green squares lined by tall mansions of rosy brick and pale stone. Sarah's eyes moved with delight over the columned porticoes, the sparkling glass and fili-greed woodwork of fanlights over paneled doors. A few minutes' walk in another direction and she and William found themselves in streets so narrow and winding the cobblestones seemed squeezed between the sagging, timbered houses. They peered through dim shop windows where pallid boys bent like old men over their work. Garbage littered the streets and open sewers ran beside.

Sarah had never imagined the sounds of London: the singsong street cries of fruit and fish peddlers, the continual clatter of wheels over cobbles, the under-brushing sound of hundreds of feet crossing and criss-crossing lanes and streets, darting through alleys. And over it all the sound of bells deep or mellow, the London church bells marking the hours from dawn to evensong until even the children sang of them:

> *Oranges and lemons,*
> *Say the bells of St. Clement's,*
> *Lend me five farthings,*
> *Say the bells of St. Martin's.*

On the morning of first rehearsal, Sarah and William reached the theatre and paused, uncertain where or how to present themselves. This was a real theatre, no barn or tavern. It stretched from Drury Lane along Brydges Street for what seemed a vast distance, and there were several entrances. Sarah reached for William's hand. Young, in love with each other and the whole wonder and excitement of their lives at this moment, they stepped inside the dark cavernous glory of the Theatre Royal in Drury Lane.

For a few moments they could see nothing. Then in the soft shimmer of light from several oil floats onstage, they began to make out the shapes of the theatre around them. They were in the house and facing the empty stage. "Sid . . . oh, Sid!" Her voice was a whisper as she moved past

William to look up at the white and gold paneled walls, the great crystal and gold chandeliers above the pit. Sarah ran her fingers caressingly over the back of a seat in the boxes — velvet! — and felt her throat tighten and tears brim up. This beautiful place! David Garrick's theatre! Now she belonged here, she and Sid.

Full of the sense of belonging, Sarah ran up onstage, shouted out an exuberant line — and heard it fall thin and lost into the emptiness. She shouted again. Again the line dwindled into echoing air. Panic surged through her. How big was this house? Her eyes probed the shadows: row on row of benches in the pit, box after box curving above them, and the galleries! — hundreds upon hundreds of seats thrusting upward until they disappeared into the great dark arch of ceiling. The place was huge; she would never be heard! As William came onstage, she turned, ran toward him — and stumbled. *This stage floor slants!* How could she ever run without falling, walk without limping? "Oh dear God, Sid, what can I do?"

Any reassurance William could give was quickly undone as the company of actors gathered, staring in open curiosity at the new actress. To William they paid little attention. They already knew he was only a bit player. But Mrs. Siddons; now that was different! Coming here to begin with a leading role, was she? Play Portia in *The Merchant of Venice,* would she? They would see. Sarah withdrew into herself as the other actresses smirked to each other, "La! How grand and aloof we are!"

Sarah stumbled through her first speeches in a half-whisper. Garrick smiled encouragingly. "Ah, well now! Portia — character you chose — on your list. So then, easy eh? Natural." The company exchanged amused glances. So! Davy had cast her in a role she picked out and this was the best she could do. Poor thing!

Stiff-necked and achy, Sarah finished the rehearsal. The next days passed in a glaze of terror. Even when William took her to Will's famous tavern for Christmas dinner, she was unable to chew more than a few bites of the crackling brown roasted goose.

Garrick, realizing that Sarah had no suitable costumes, suggested she choose one from the theatre's stock. She found a saque-back gown in her favorite color, salmon pink. Feeling cheered, she accepted William's repetition of the old actors' phrase, Everything Will Be All Right on the Night. The Night was Friday, December 29, 1775. The playbills announced her in customary fashion with new actors as "A Young Lady (her first appearance)." Critics and theatre buffs knew that the Young Lady was Mrs. Siddons, David Garrick's newest find from the provincial theatres.

Sarah waited in the wings, her legs trembling, her throat dry. The cue came. Stiff-legged with fright, trying to hold herself straight on the raked stage, she entered into a blast of light that struck her from all sides. Accustomed to the soft light of candles and floats, she now faced Garrick's famous side lighting. From each of the wings, the brilliance of many candles backed by metal shields reflected an intensified light onto the stage. She groped blindly and spoke her first words in a harsh, feeble voice. Mr. Benseley played more vigorously, carrying the scene almost alone as Sarah's voice shook and dropped to a whisper at the ends of her lines. The pit audience stirred restlessly. At last in Portia's famous Quality of Mercy speech, Sarah regained her voice control. She recalled her mother's instructions and strove to intone the words and phrases correctly.

The next morning, as Sarah nursed the baby, William read the notices. "Here's one that says you were pretty!"

"What else does it say? Read it all."

William sighed. "It says, 'On before us tottered rather than walked, a very pretty, delicate, fragile-looking creature, dressed in a most unbecoming manner . . . uncertain whereabouts to fix either her eyes or her feet . . . at the close of a sentence her words generally lapsed into a horrid whisper.'" Gloomily, William searched for more flattering words. He found only comments that Sarah's voice was inadequate, her costume frightful.

Sarah picked up another paper. Mr. Woodfall of the *Morning Chronicle* wrote that he "understood that the new Portia had been the heroine of one of those petty parties of travelling comedians which wander over the country," and suggested it had been a mistake for her to leave them. He admitted she delivered her words sensibly, then added: "Every allowance being made, we advise her to throw more fire and spirit into her performance. She cannot be too early informed, that on the stage nothing is so barren of either profit or fame as a cold *correctness.*"

For a while they sat, bleakly silent. William tried to encourage her. He would help, he promised. He would coach her. David Garrick took the same view. Work. That was the thing. He would help her, teach her. In the green-room where the company gathered for gossip or cards between scenes and where Garrick held some of his play discussions, he made it plain to his actors that he held Sarah in high regard. With a brief bow to her where she sat in the corner, he conducted her to a chair beside him.

In his revival of the Jubilee Pageant first done at Stratford-on-Avon, he cast Sarah as Venus. Immediately the other actresses sneered, "Ha! *Garrick's* Venus!" The night of performance she and seven-year-old Tom Dibdin as Cupid began their rehearsed move across stage during a crowd scene. Suddenly they felt themselves pushed backward. Sarah held tightly to Tom's hand. She was helpless against the crowd shoving and jostling them into the wings. Garrick appeared beside her and, bowing, led her down to the footlights. Near tears herself, she bent over the frightened little boy. "Smile, Tom, as Mr. Garrick told you. If you will keep on smiling no matter what happens, I'll give you a whole bag of sugar-plums. Your favorite kind." She kept her promise, and from that night on Tom Dibdin remained her friend — and almost her only friend at Drury Lane.

Garrick next cast Sarah in the name role of *Epicoene*, a breeches part. Again she read in the reviews that she lacked that essential of great acting — fire. In fact, said the *Chronicle,* she was "entirely destitute of the natural fire." She was shortly replaced in the part by a young man.

Yet Garrick's faith seemed undiminished. He cast her as Julia in a new operatic comedy by the Reverend Mr. Bate.

In spite of his title, Parson Bate had fought a good number of duels, "thrashed" several men who had offended him, and been accused of libeling others. The audience was not entirely made up of well-wishers. Quite a few came with the small tin whistles known as catcalls hidden under their coats. But Garrick's sumptuous production seemed to calm them, and opening night passed off fairly smoothly. Sarah's reviews, however, were harsh. Said one paper, she "rendered that ridiculous which the author evidently intended to be pleasant." And Sarah, who loved playing comedy, read that she had "no comedy in her nature." No fire and no comedy. She began to panic.

As he had promised, David Garrick worked with her, tutoring her privately, giving her extra attention in rehearsals. In her panic each suggestion he made seemed an attack. She had been acting for years. What was so wrong now? Garrick's constantly repeated "from Nature! Hey, now! Real — make it real" only confused her. Nevertheless, she tried to follow his instructions to observe, to watch everyone and everything, to remember and store up her impressions. It was, he told her, the key to making characters real and vital. He related how he walked through the streets just watching people, how he accompanied his newspaper friends to trials, fires, accidents, observing the ways in which real people expressed themselves in the heat of crisis.

Sarah walked the streets of the theatre district, through the huge open square of Covent Garden, observing the faces of apple-sellers, charwomen, and the fashionable ladies who paraded the arcaded piazza along the north and east sides of the square. She stood before the Theatre Royal in Covent Garden and wondered how it might have gone for her there. And sometimes she went along tree-lined Inigo Lane and into the simple austerity of St. Paul's, "the actors' church."

She walked the poorer districts and became haunted by what she saw: poverty unimagined in her country days. Was this the cost of failure? This sick, toothless, young old-age in peddlers and market women, the twisted bodies and bitter faces of children who lived by picking pockets or who died as "parish children" in miserable orphanages? Shaken and frightened, she refused the thought of failure. She would not let this happen to her and her children! If the critics were against her, the fault was not in her; it was in David Garrick. She grew stubborn, and bucked harder against the threat that Garrick's lessons seemed. Yet there were times when she adored him.

On the fourth night of Parson Bate's play, a gang of the author's prizefighter friends confronted his enemies who wanted the show pulled from the boards. Open fighting broke out. Shrieking ladies scrambled to get out of the theatre and were tripped by their massive hoops. Garrick stopped the show and stepped to the footlights. An orange was flung at him, then a lighted candle looped onto the stage. Instantly an actor smothered it. All actors lived in terror of backstage fire, speeding through the flimsy material of costumes and sets and old wooden buildings. Yet Garrick remained calm, faced the crowd smiling and announced that the author had fled the theatre with his manuscript. The play would not be acted again. "But suffer me to say this: my theatrical life will be short, and I wish to end it in peace." Disarmed by his unflurried coolness, the rioters dispersed. Who but David Garrick, Sarah thought, could have faced this threat to his theatre with such charm and courage?

Garrick gave her a place in the boxes from which she could watch on nights when she was not acting. Observe them all, he said, Mrs. Abington, Mrs. Yates, Miss Younge. Watch, judge, learn! Instead she watched David Garrick. England's greatest actor! Sarah was sure there could be none greater. Every word he spoke, every move he made was truth itself. Yet a truth unnoticed by the average eye until Garrick, by his use of it, revealed what had been hidden. The smallest detail was always right — the angle of a wig when he came home drunk, the sag of a garter, the slight moonfaced grin, the stricken voice when as Hamlet he saw his father's ghost. She wished he were her father, or an older brother, someone to whom she belonged, could call Davy, could really talk to without being afraid. And yet in rehearsals she became more defensive. How could she ever equal acting like his or measure up to his demands?

Once again, to the surprise of the company, Garrick cast Sarah in a good part, that of Emily in a new comedy, *The Runaway*. The ladies of the company watched rehearsals with glee-tinged jealousy and snide remarks: *Poor dear had best do as Mr. Woodfall said and get back to her barns! Did Davy think he could make another Peg Woffington of this blundering country actress? Hah!* Sarah was aware of the comments, aware that David Garrick had once loved the tall, auburn-haired Woffington whose brilliant comedy had won all London's heart. But he had no right to make her into someone else! Not even Woffington! Angry and upset, Sarah played Emily as best she could. The reviewers hardly noticed.

Backstage, gossip continued: Garrick had hired her only to chasten majestic Mrs. Yates, stately Miss Younge and the fashion-setting Abington. Sarah began to wonder. Was it true? Garrick cast her in still another comedy as his young wife in *The Suspicious Husband*. Stung to fury, the other young actresses muttered in her hearing that of course Davy would cast Mrs. Siddons. Having no ability, she would never put him in the shadow.

Sarah rehearsed determinedly with Garrick on the role. A critic had scored her awkward use of her arms. They would work on it, said Garrick. Sarah flung her arms wide. "Ah, come now — naturally," insisted Garrick. Sarah tried again. Better. But as she went through the scene once more she resumed the wide gestures of her touring days. Garrick sighed. "If you wave your arms about in that fashion you will knock off my wig!"

"Afraid I will overshadow your nose?" Sarah snapped before she thought. Garrick's black eyebrows soared, then he burst into laughter. In performance one critic noted that Sarah was "by no means inferior"; the other reviewers thought her not worth mentioning.

Having announced that he would retire when the season ended, Garrick now played one performance of each of his famous roles. But he announced that he would play *Richard III* several times and once as a Royal Command Performance. He debated his casting of Lady Anne. Miss Sherry and Miss

David Garrick. Engraving after a portrait by Sir Joshua Reynolds. (From the Raymond Mander and Joe Mitchenson Theatre Collection)

Greville had both played the role — should it be one of them? Or Mrs. Siddons? He thought back to the morning at Guy's Cliffe. Had his judgment been betrayed by that momentary resemblance to his once-beloved Woffington? He sighed. There would never be another lovely Peggy. Why not give Mrs. Siddons a chance in tragedy. He cast her as Lady Anne.

He rehearsed with Sarah carefully. He himself was keyed to an unusual pitch of tension. This was his greatest role, these few performances his last on any stage. Sarah knew that to be chosen as his Lady Anne was a coveted honor. She was so frightened that on opening night she forgot his directions and did the opposite of what he had told her. Nonetheless she opened the morning papers with much hope. She read that Mrs. Siddons was "a lamentable Lady Anne" and even William's reminder that the papers had also said Mrs. Johnston was "a frightful Duchess" failed to cheer her.

What would happen now? Would Garrick recommend her to the new management? She hardly dared ask, but when one afternoon she was called to David Garrick's office she tried to speak of it. He waved her quiet. He could promise nothing, he said, the new managers would make the decision, but he would recommend her. To seal the bargain he pulled out a treasured folio copy of Shakespeare's plays. Sarah noted the date: 1623 — it must be one of Garrick's most valued possessions! "We shall both sign it," he said quickly. "Testimony, eh? Your merit — my obligation." When they had both written their names, Garrick handed the folio to Sarah. "Well now! Keep it. It is yours." Unable to speak, she took the precious folio. At the door she made a sudden small curtsy and was gone.

The season over, William and Sarah bundled the children into a stagecoach and set out for Birmingham. Unable to afford a summer holiday, they had accepted Joseph Younger's offer to play in the larger towns of his circuit, and the industrial cities of Liverpool and Birmingham. Sarah was to play leading roles on the circuit and her name would command large letters on the playbill. She was a London actress who had played with David Garrick. Certain that in spite of her poor reviews she would return to London in October, Sarah began the summer happily.

It was an afternoon in August when she came home to find William pale with shock. The children?

"Sid! Sid, what's happened? Is it Sally? Henry?'"

He touched an open letter on the table. "From Mr. Hopkins, the prompter. An official letter. Your services are no longer required by the Theatre Royal in Drury Lane."

Sarah snatched up the letter, read it, then read it again. In spite of Garrick's promise she had been fired. "I don't believe it! *I do not believe it!*" But it was true. The dream was over — and she was twenty-one.

In London only one of the Drury Lane company failed to cheer the new managers' decision. Said the elegant Frances Abington, "They are fools!"

Chapter Four

A Worthless Candidate
for Fame and Fortune

WILLIAM WAS FRANKLY DELIGHTED when they returned
to the provincial theatres where he could act as before.
The winter in London had been a bitter one for him.
Sarah might not have gotten just the roles she wanted,
or the accolades of the critics, but at least she had acted.
William had merely walked on as one of a crowd of
soldiers or street beggars, or helped backstage with
properties and sets. His name had not once been on the
playbills, and after the first few weeks he had been
dropped from the paybook and the total of their salaries paid to Sarah. But he soon discovered that even
in the provincial theatres it was now Mrs. Siddons the
managers wanted; they permitted William to accompany her.

In Birmingham, Sarah was immediately cast in

leading roles. Playing opposite her in the male leads was John Henderson, a homely man, sensitive, intelligent and enchanted with Sarah. Henderson had earned great popularity in leading roles at the Theatre Royal in Bath, and come October he was scheduled to assume many of David Garrick's roles in London.

Working with him was pure joy for Sarah. As Henderson spoke his lines, every word sounded as real and natural as if he had just that moment thought of it. Yet his thinking seemed more original, quicker in imagery than the average man's. When Henderson spoke to her Sarah found herself answering him directly and naturally. She was reminded of that long-ago moment at Guy's Cliffe when she had found herself speaking directly to Garrick, unable to look away.

Henderson, like Garrick, was excited about acting. "Look for the images in your own mind," he would say. "See them. Really see them! Enjoy them. Cry over them. Then let them have your voice." Back and forth Henderson and Sarah tossed their lines, giving them new meanings, letting laughter curl around the words, or sorrow or pleading. This was what Garrick had meant! But Henderson was not yet famous; with him Sarah could relax, listen and learn.

When he heard the news of Sarah's dismissal from Drury Lane, Henderson promptly sent off a letter to John Palmer, manager of the theatre at Bath, urging that Palmer engage her at once. Palmer was pleased to hear from his friend and former actor, but he had no place for Mrs. Siddons. He would keep her in mind for the future.

As Sarah's first disbelief wore off, she faced the fact but

not the truth of her dismissal. Her mind twisted away from any thought that she had failed. She snatched up the shoddy bits of remembered backstage gossip: Garrick's teaching, the hours he spent working with her in rehearsal, the loan of his box, were done only to annoy his temperamental leading ladies, Younge, Yates and Abington. Garrick had cast her in no roles where she could win distinction because he was jealous of her. David Garrick had used her and betrayed her. She repeated it to William, to Henderson, to herself. Yet her innate honesty refused that answer.

"Banished from Drury Lane . . . a worthless candidate for fame and fortune." Years later, secure in her fame, she could openly use these words about herself. Now she could only think them, and try to fight them down. She had two children to support — and William. There was no evading that truth any longer. William was that worst of all things for an actor to be: he was adequate. Not bad enough to be interesting, not good enough to be exciting. If the Siddons family were to survive it was up to Sarah. She dared not be a failure!

Silently, alone, she fought the inward battle until she was exhausted and sick. It was useless for anyone to point out to her that the new managers were quite at liberty to choose the actors they wanted and ignore anyone's recommendation.

William watched her grow thinner, more drawn. "Sally, you have got to eat more," he insisted. "You need a tonic. They say a pint of port wine taken with each meal . . ."

"You're mad. I should go onstage reeling drunk."

William fussed and fumed. He told her everyone supposed her to be going into a decline. She ignored him. There

was no time for a decline. Mr. Younger wanted her to stay
on for the winter season. She agreed. And the work began
the cure.

In the effort to subdue her inner conflict Sarah worked
with new drive and concentration. She played her comic
characters as she would like to be, high-hearted, untroubled
and free. When she played tragedy, some of her own bitterness and fury bit through the lines of the character. Things
she could never express to cautious, unhappy William she
let pour out in the tears and storms of her characters. Years
later, she would be able to look back from a more sophisticated knowledge of her art and say that "she had often got
credit for the truth and feeling of her acting when she was
doing nothing more than relieve her heart of its own grief."
While she was still on Yates and Younger's circuit she understood little beyond the fact that her acting was taking on
the indefinable quality of fire that London critics had found
lacking, and that audiences were responding with more than
the cheers and whoops they gave to any attractive girl whose
legs they could admire in breeches parts.

There was criticism still, some of it crudely stated. The
advice of the galleries in Manchester was that Mrs. Siddons
"motions nicely but she can't shout out loud." Sarah tried,
but still frail in health, she lacked the physical strength to
project full voice.

One winter morning Sarah entered the theatre in Liverpool to hear a woman's voice fairly shaking the rafters in
its raging resonance. She saw a tall, golden-haired young
woman, storming at a timid weary man who leaned against

the wall, unable to get in a defensive word. Suddenly the fury spent itself and Sarah was confronted by a pair of measuring, pleasant eyes. "G-g-good morning!" said the young woman, extending her hand, "I am Elizabeth In-in-inchbald."

Sarah's new friendship with Elizabeth Inchbald was to be a long one. They could talk together easily and intimately of acting and children, ideas and problems. Elizabeth's husband, at whom her flaring temper was often directed, was, like William, a bit-part actor some years older than his wife. The two couples became close friends, and once again Sarah felt the security of working with people she liked and trusted. She felt even more secure when in the winter of 1777–1778 her brother John Philip turned up. The priesthood was not for him, he said; where could he find a stage to act on? John was quickly absorbed into the Younger company and the Siddons-Inchbald friendship.

As Sarah learned to know Elizabeth Inchbald she began to understand how protected she herself had been, by her parents in the Kemble company, by the Greatheeds at Guy's Cliffe and by William. Elizabeth had no such background. She had gone alone to London as a stagestruck teen-ager determined to find a theatre job despite her stammer. Unprepared for a city where crime was commonplace in the streets, she had spent days and nights running from real and imagined pursuit by thugs and procurers. She found cheap shelter where she could, until at last she secured an interview with a theatrical producer who smilingly tried to rape her. Forever after, Elizabeth Inchbald would fear men and poverty. And Sarah for the first time questioned whether her own reactions to criticism and competition in London had not been oversensitive. Her letters to friends took on a new determination. The time would come, she told them, when they would hear of her again.

In March the Siddonses, Inchbalds, John Philip and two young actors from the company spent a month's holiday together in the country. At a farm on Russell Moor near Appledurcombe the group lived as the newer poets and writers of the time advised. Live naturally and simply, forget the rules of established society and be as children once again — this was the poets' cry. The young actors, wearing old clothes, playing on the moors with four-year-old Henry and two-year-old Sally, thoroughly enjoyed the holiday. For the first time in several years, Sarah let down her wall of defensive dignity, laughed and sang with the others as they shared cooking, washing and ironing, or an evening's game of cards. Sometimes she and John Philip sang comic duets; occasionally she watched as the children played with the tiny stage properties and furniture John and Elizabeth made for them from bits of wire, thread, paper and scraps of cloth. A visitor to the farm told of finding Sarah in the kitchen one morning, singing as she fed Sally and Henry and occasionally sharing a spoonful of their bread and milk.

When Sarah received an offer from Tate Wilkinson, the holiday was over. In the hierarchy of theatres outside London, Tate's York circuit rated high. A vain, capable, tough veteran of the London theatre, a brilliant mimic but never a great actor, Tate had decided to leave the city and use his knowledge as a country manager. He could boast that his costumes and scenery were better than any outside London with the possible exception of the Theatre Royal at Bath. He had been hearing of the beautiful young Mrs. Siddons. Would she join his company for a month's engagement in York?

William was elated. This was indeed an important step forward. Second in importance to Canterbury as a center of the English Church, York was growing in importance as a marketing and manufacturing town. To Sarah a York engagement meant new audiences and critics and a new theatre company. The offer fed her determination to make good, to earn more money for her family — and it touched off her fears.

Jovial Tate Wilkinson was puzzled by his new actress and a bit alarmed. She was so thin, so fragile, could she possibly hold up under the strain of performing leading roles? Why should a girl as young and beautiful as Mrs. Siddons display such aloofness when he introduced her to the other players? He invited her to his home and there, over a dinner of roast mutton and dark brown country ale, he let the motherly Mrs. Wilkinson take over. Soon his stiff young actress was laughing and talking easily.

"You'll be missing London, I daresay," ventured Mrs. Wilkinson, as Tate poured more ale.

"No." Sarah took a deep gulp from the foaming glass. "Oh, I do love ale!" she said, half in apology.

"There's more!" Tate laughed. "Now tell us . . ." and he began a gentle questioning, encouraging her to talk of

London and Drury Lane, Garrick and the ladies Yates, Younge and Abington. He listened to her brief replies, and watched her stiffen again. So that was it, her pride had been scored and something deeper, too.

Sarah was speaking to Mrs. Wilkinson. "I like the country so much better! The friendliness, the courtesies I meet with. . . ."

"It was cruel treatment you had in London," Tate suggested.

"Cruel and unjust! I never want to play there again!"

"Then shall we discuss the parts you'll play here? Now, to open, you will have Euphrasia in *The Grecian Daughter*. And I," said Tate with a small bow, "shall have the honor of playing your old father." He pulled a small enameled snuffbox from his waistcoat pocket, carefully took a pinch between his thumb and forefinger and placed it on the back of his left hand. "My favorite Irish blend," he said, then paused. "Do you, by any chance, snuff, Mrs. Siddons?"

Sarah reddened slightly. Snuffing was not considered ladylike, but the truth was she loved it. She nodded and took a pinch. In companionable silence they lifted the snuff to their nostrils and inhaled it happily, before continuing their discussion of Sarah's roles.

Tate shrewdly cast Sarah in the roles of persecuted, suffering heroines through whom she could live out the hurt within herself. For balance, he gave her a few comedy parts in which the girl who loved food and drink and beautiful clothes might come alive. Tate's judgment was vindicated in cheering houses and critical acclaim. Mr. Cornelius Swann, who considered himself a most exacting critic, praised Sarah lavishly, and added that the grace with which she died in *Aspasia* was "so elegant."

Wilkinson spoke of Sarah's work in terms that were balm to an actress who had been criticized for lacking fire. Mrs. Siddons, said Tate, "was a lamp not to be extinguished"; she had "an unquenchable flame of soul." There were repercussions backstage. Sarah hid any tension she felt behind a mask of dignity as her predecessor, Mrs. Glassington, was rapidly forgotten and her rival, Mrs. Hudson, resigned in a fit of hysterics.

The month over, Wilkinson asked Sarah to continue with his company. Knowing her joy in the silver-trimmed costume he had provided her for Lady Alton — "I wish I could keep it always, it makes me feel so happy" — he offered to give her costumes more beautiful than anything Mr. Younger could match. Sarah was tempted, but having promised Younger she would return to his company when her month in York was over, she went back to Manchester.

Once again, the Siddonses resumed touring, piling children, luggage and costumes into a post chaise at two or three o'clock in the morning, stopping for breakfast at some roadside inn, then into the chaise again while fresh horses pounded them along the road to their destination. In the comfortable style they had adopted, the Inchbalds, Siddonses and John Philip took lodgings together, and were constantly in and out of each other's rooms. John worked with Elizabeth on lines, Mr. Inchbald painted in Sarah's room while she lay in bed ill, William roamed back and forth reading or napping.

These casual living arrangements inevitably drew the notice of more conventional people. In Birmingham, a disapproving townsman informed against them as being rogues and vagabonds. In her usual tart fashion, Elizabeth Inchbald noted the outcome in her journal: "Their worships the magistrates, in their sagacity, not wiser than the laws, though perhaps wishing they had alike been permitted to sleep together, stopped the performances." Sarah, William and John Philip left for Wolverhampton, and by the following June they were again in Liverpool.

It was June of 1778, two years after Sarah had left London. Liverpool was a port city, conscious of its importance to English shipping. Audiences wanted no more of country actors; they demanded that Younger bring only actors who had played before the King. Sarah had played before King George on Garrick's Royal Command night, but it was not enough. Opening night found a howling, stamping audience in the house. When Mr. Younger stepped before the curtain he was driven back by hisses and jeers, potatoes, hats and bottles. He retired backstage. As John Philip wrote to Elizabeth Inchbald, William was then equipped "with a board large enough to secure his person, inscribed with Mr. Younger's petition to be heard. The rogues would hear nothing, and Siddons may thank his wooden protector that his bones were whole."

Bottles crashed against the back wall and bounced off William's chest. The actors decided to proceed with the play.

Perhaps that might calm the fury. The uproar increased. As a broken bottle whizzed past her face, Mrs. Kniveton slid to the floor in a faint, hoops flopping and ruffled underdrawers showing. The audience whooped with laughter as she was dragged hastily into the wings. They began climbing up onto the stage, fanning the candles out with their hats. Terrified of fire, Sarah, William and the other actors fled from the scene. Satisfied, the rioters scooped their money from the box-office till and tramped out of the theatre.

The following week William received a letter from Bath. He read it quickly, his smile widening with each line. "Sally! It's from John Palmer. He wants you for next season."

"At Bath?" This was the theatre where John Henderson had played. This was the theatre known to be a stepping-stone to London, second only to London in importance. Sarah hesitated. "What of you, Sid? Will he take you, too?"

William shrugged. "For bit parts. You're the one he wants, Sally. He says that his prompter, Mr. Floor, saw you here in Liverpool and added his strong recommendation to that of John Henderson. Sally — this is the Theatre Royal in Bath, the only theatre outside London producing under a Royal Patent from the King. You must accept."

"Yes. I want to." Now she was ready. Two years had passed since that bleak notice dismissing her from Drury Lane. Two years of fighting the inner accusation of failure. Now she must try herself out on a new audience, a highly critical one, and new theatre reviewers as sharp and knowledgeable as London men. "I want to very much."

Chapter Five

33 Paragon Street

AT LAST, after two and a half years of touring, the Siddonses could settle into lodgings for more than a fortnight. The trunks could be stowed in the cellar. The children could sleep the nights through and not be pulled from their beds and bundled into a stagecoach at three o'clock in the morning.

Her arm around three-year-old Sally, Sarah stood in the window looking at the cobbled street below. How clean it was in the soft October sunlight. How quiet. How different from London. Tobias Smollett, the novelist, might sneer that Bath was "a stew-pan of idleness and insignificance," but John Henderson had said that his experience before the knowledgeable Bath audience was "a college" where he had learned to perfect his art. Sarah hugged her daughter close. Why not forget London and stay here always in a town where children could play in safety on the tranquil banks of the Avon?

Sarah already knew that there would be no idleness for her in Bath. She had seen Palmer's schedule for her; there was hard and steady work ahead in the playhouse on Orchard Street. For the second time in her life she would be acting in a Theatre Royal, the only one outside London. And the old questions and conflicts stirred. What exactly had gone wrong in London? Would it happen again? She knew that she was a better actress now; just why and how she was remained a matter of uncertainty.

The work began immediately. Mr. Palmer managed a theatre in nearby Bristol as well as the more famous one in Bath. His actors ranged between them, playing in Bath on Tuesdays, Thursdays and Saturdays, then making the two- to three-hour stagecoach journey to Bristol to play on the alternate nights. As the newest actress in the company, Sarah was assigned Thursday as the night on which she would regularly play leading roles in Bath.

She opened her season on October 24 as Lady Townly, a comedy part in which she had been greatly applauded on the York circuit. In Bath there was scarcely anyone in the house to applaud. Sarah learned that Thursday was Cotillion Night, when as James Boaden the theatre critic had remarked, "everything that could move" went to the Lower Assembly Rooms to dance. The following Thursday, Sarah again played in a comedy, and again to a very thin house. However, Mrs. Thrale, a friend of the famous Dr. Samuel Johnson, attended this performance and spoke afterward to her many acquaintances of the new actress's "significant looks."

For her third leading role, Sarah played Elwina in the tragedy *Percy*. The next morning, the Bath *Chronicle* reviewer was ecstatic and Sarah read that she "was established in the judgement of the town as the most capital actress that has performed here in many years." Her luck had turned. Her season had begun.

Soon, over the books at Tennant's Library, under the crystal chandeliers of the Pump Room, the gossip was all of the beautiful, frail young actress with the staid, fair-haired husband and those two charming children. Now it was the Cotillion that had thin houses. They could dance another night, said the residents of Bath; on Thursday night they *must* see Mrs. Siddons. Fortunately for Mr. Palmer, he had enlarged his theatre during the past summer. Sarah was filling the house.

Occasionally, William played small parts with the company. When Sarah played Hamlet for a one-night experiment he played Guildenstern; when she was cast as Jane Shore he played the five-line part of Derby. But more and more William played only the role of Mrs. Siddons' husband. He and Sarah were, in fact, beginning to switch traditional real-life roles. She supported the family while he stayed home, played cards with friends, or strolled along Paragon Street.

Palmer required that his leading actors play supporting roles when needed. As a result, Sarah's week often began with a rush from the Monday rehearsal at Bath to catch the stagecoach for Bristol where she played Monday evening. Tuesday she was back in Bath for the performance there. Wednesday she played Bristol again, often leaving directly after her performance for the return trip to Bath on the night coach. Long after midnight she returned home to gain a few hours' rest before her important Thursday night performance in Bath. Friday was Bristol again and back to Bath for Saturday night's performance, frequently in a leading role. As the season progressed, Sarah was often too exhausted to care what role she played and referred to it only as "some fatiguing part."

But she was learning. John Henderson had been right. The comments she received, the criticism and applause given her by the perceptive Bath audience taught her much. Her very exhaustion meant that she must, to play well as she was determined to do, concentrate all her energies onstage within the character. She put aside the country actor's tendency to flirt with the audience, to trick them into this or that reaction. She was learning to play with sharp intelligence and spontaneity. Her ear was becoming attuned to the various pitches of real life, her voice responsive to the feeling she recognized. Bath audiences would accept no less.

Once they approved a player, however, these people were openly friendly. Warmed by their response, Sarah relaxed and played with more zest than ever before. Or so she felt. Sometimes she caught herself wishing that David Garrick could see her, tell her whether she was working the right way now or not. If only she could hear his "Aha! Well, now, that's the way of it!" she would know.

Interior of the Theatre Royal, Bath.
(From the Raymond Mander
and Joe Mitchenson Theatre Collection)

In November, John Henderson came up from London for a short visit, and on November 17, he acted Hamlet with Sarah as his Queen Gertrude. As before, she responded to the directness and reality of his playing with an answering reality of her own.

Two nights later, Sarah acted again with Henderson in *The Merchant of Venice.* Waiting offstage for her cue, she only half-listened as Henderson began one of Shylock's speeches. She had heard it so many times before, she knew it by heart. Suddenly, she began to listen with her whole mind and body tensed, responding, thinking as it had never occurred to her to think about Shylock, about what it meant to be a Jew. Henderson spoke the words quietly:

> *You call me misbeliever, cut-throat dog,*
> *And spit upon my Jewish gaberdine,*

and Sarah wanted to reach out, to touch him, somehow to comfort the hurt behind the dignity. Know that speech by heart? Never until now.

When Sarah, as Portia, began the famous speech,

> *The quality of mercy is not strained* . . .

it was no recitation of unfelt words. She had no consciousness of the correct vowel sounds, of whether the audience was impressed by her acting or not. She was pleading for the life of a man who intended no wrong, for the cause of life itself above the dry dictates of justice. The walls of the theatre reverberated with applause.

Back in London, John Henderson wasted no time in seeing Richard Brinsley Sheridan, his manager at Drury Lane. "Brinsley, I swear, Mrs. Siddons has never had an equal, and she will never have a superior."

Sheridan sipped his coffee. "That was said of David Garrick, that he would never have an equal or superior. Remember?"

Henderson reddened. He was trying and not yet succeeding in becoming Garrick's superior. "No matter. You will regret it if Covent Garden engages her first."

"So my father tells me. But her London reviews were dreadful, John. Let her stay in Bath awhile longer." Sheridan smiled. "My father will continue to watch her."

Old Thomas Sheridan was indeed watching Sarah, with both admiration and amazement. To please David Garrick, he had attended several of Sarah's London performances and thought her very poor. Finally, at Bath, after hearing constantly that young Mrs. Siddons was a "great genius" and an "astonishing tragedian," he had gone to a performance. Then, like the rest of Bath, he had attended her plays more and more frequently. He watched her with the critical eyes of a man who had spent his life in theatre, and he nodded approvingly. Davy was right, he thought, and Davy had taught her well.

But David Garrick would never see her act again. He died on January 20, 1779. Old Mr. Sheridan told her about it later. "Ah, yes," he mused, "the Bishop of Rochester himself received the body at the West Door — Westminster Abbey, of course. Davy was laid to rest in the Poet's Corner.

There was the music of that great funeral service Purcell wrote, and mind you, a full chorus of voices. The Duke of Devonshire was one of the pallbearers, and the Earls of Camden and Spencer. Great men to be carrying a player to his grave. And old Dr. Johnson following the coffin. . . ."

Sarah listened, her throat tight. How strange, she thought, that Samuel Johnson — he must be very old by now — should see Davy buried before him. She remembered Garrick's story of how as a boy he had been a student of Dr. Johnson's, and the two of them had walked to London from the country, sharing the few pennies they had between them. Johnson was determined that Garrick should get the chance his talents demanded. Dear God, how could the old man have borne it, to walk behind that coffin, to see David Garrick buried?

"He thought well of you, you know." Mr. Sheridan nodded, hearing the past. "He said to me once, 'You will see, she possesses enough powers to delight and electrify an audience.'"

"Davy" — Sarah's voice shook — "said that about me?"

"Aye. It was after I'd seen you in *The Runaway*. I'd thought you very bad."

"I was." That was the truth of it. Suddenly she was crying, a storm of bitterness released. Knowing at last that Garrick had not used her or betrayed her, she could forgive herself for failure.

On the first of May, Sarah stepped to the front of the stage after her performance. Speaking quietly, yet emotionally, her whole heart behind her words, she gave the lines of Brinsley Sheridan's "Monody on Garrick." And her audience wept with her.

A month later Sarah finished her first season at Bath, and William promptly signed her contract for the next. It had been, she felt, the best year she had ever spent. She had faced a difficult audience and discerning critics and won them both, had worked under new management and succeeded. And on February 24, she and William had stood beneath the great fan-vaulted roof of Bath Abbey church as their third child, a daughter, was christened Maria.

It had been luck, Sarah thought, that most of her casting that winter was in tragedy. Pregnant, she found it impossible to move as lightly and quickly as comedy required. But — thank heaven for hoop skirts — she could go on working until almost time for the birth. Some of her audience, of course, realized her pregnancy. Some, like the Reverend Mr. Whalley and his wife, began to worry about the fragile-looking girl and sent wine, fresh farm eggs and fruit to build up her strength. Bath audiences told her in every possible way, with huge attendance at her Thursday nights, with gifts, with warm interest, that they wished her well.

". . . and your Benefit brought me over a hundred pounds." William was happily counting up their earnings for the year. Sarah nodded. That meant she could rest for the summer, have time for the children, time to get acquainted with her own baby. And time to think.

She was beginning to know, she told William as they lay stretched at ease on the summer-green banks of the Avon, what it meant to "act from Nature" as Garrick had, freely and spontaneously. William became grumpy. There were certain gestures for certain emotions and that was that. It was the way he had been taught, and it was right. No need for all this watching people.

Sarah smiled and continued to watch the passersby. Let Sid sputter if he must. She would go on observing more and more deeply, noting the immense range of difference in the gestures and tones that expressed what people felt and who they were. She would watch the women, young and old, aristocrats and paper sellers, seeing each as a separate human being. Fascinated, she would study how they revealed their stations in life, their sickness or health, their anger or joy in the way they used their bodies and voices. Let William stay with the old rules if he wished. She knew now what kind of actress she wanted to be, and that she had at last begun the learning.

When Sarah opened her next season, familiar faces appeared in her audiences, welcoming her as a friend. But as before, Bath audiences were critical and knowing. They watched with eager expectancy for the signs of developing talent. They saw Sarah begin to introduce experiments, small human touches in her characters that she had observed in real people. And by their applause or silence these audiences gave her the measure of her reach and a sense of distance still to be covered.

Sarah was now studying as she never had before. On her evenings off, 33 Paragon Street resounded alternately with shouts of laughter as she played with the children or her own increasingly rich tones as she practiced the voice exercises old Mr. Sheridan had taught her. Later, after she had said evening prayers with the children and seen them to bed, Sarah read and reread the plays she had long known, searching for new meanings in the lines.

The result of this concentrated work was a season in which Sarah gained the admiration of new and powerful friends, among them Georgianna, Duchess of Devonshire. "Mrs. Siddons," said the Duchess firmly, "belongs in London. What can Brinsley Sheridan be thinking of not to have her at Drury Lane?" When she returned to London, she put statement and question directly before young Sheridan.

And Richard Brinsley Sheridan listened. Now twenty-nine, he had been for the past four years acknowledged the wittiest of England's living playwrights. With the profits from his plays and the credit his fame accrued he had bought the Theatre Royal in Drury Lane and taken over the management. But theatre was not enough: he turned to politics. For the past year he had put his writing talents at the service of the liberal Whig party, and had begun to have hopes of running for Parliament. He was a frequent visitor at Devonshire House, for the Duke shared his opinion that the war against the American colonies was stupid folly and the colonists were only asserting their rights as free men to live as they chose. Sheridan had learned to know the Duchess of Devonshire well, and he respected her opinions.

Sheridan thought it over; the Duchess, John Henderson, his own father — three whose judgment he valued — were all urging him to engage Mrs. Siddons at once. He took up his pen, began to make notes on salary, possible roles, terms of employment. Best let his father approach her, he decided. That would keep the matter quiet and not alert rival Covent Garden.

While Sarah debated her answer, news hit Bath of trouble in London. William rattled his morning newspaper in agitation. Meeting in High Street shops, people spoke in worried tones: *But, my dear, there's been rioting and burning for two nights! The mob rules! We shall have revolution! They're attacking and beating Catholics on the streets! The government is doing nothing!*

Attacking Catholics? Sarah began to listen. Her father and John Philip were Catholics. Sarah knew vaguely that there had been rules since Cromwell's time a hundred years before that denied Catholics some of the rights of other Englishmen, but why were Catholics being beaten in the London streets?

Hurrying home, Sarah snatched up the papers and began to fire questions at the surprised William. Lord George Gordon, he explained, was leading an uprising against the new laws Parliament was considering, laws to free Catholics from the old strictures against them.

"But that's only fair!" Sarah burst out. "Catholics serve in the army and navy. They pay the same taxes on their gin! Why shouldn't they have the same rights as other Englishmen?"

William sighed. How could he explain when he was not sure he understood it himself? But if Sarah were beginning to take an interest in politics, at least he should try. Gordon's Protestant Association, he told her, was rigid in its demands that Protestants remain a favored group. The members had started rumors that if Catholics were given equality the Pope would rule England and the Inquisition would put Protestants to torture. There were pamphlets out, *The Thunderer* and *England in Blood,* saying that already Catholics were secreting arms and weapons, making ready to burn heretics in Covent Garden Square.

Sarah was aghast. It was ridiculous. The idea of John Philip or her jovial father lighting fires under heretics! How could people believe these things? But people were believing them; and the burning and killing continued.

Terrified people escaping their London homes brought eyewitness news to Bath. Catholic churches were being invaded by mobs who looted them and set them afire. Homes of prominent Catholics were put to the torch. The Mansfields had barely escaped with their lives as a mob smashed furniture and burned the books and manuscripts that were Lord Mansfield's life work. Thirty-six major fires had raged unchecked during a two-hour period one night. Firemen and troops were helpless. Private citizens were equally helpless before the surging mobs demanding food, money, weapons. A knock on the door, a shouted demand, and if the demand were not met, the householder was beaten, his family left shivering on the street to watch their home reduced to ashes.

News poured in. The Palaces were threatened, the Mint, the Bank. Four prisons had been attacked and Newgate burned, its prisoners released. Some of them, in more terror of the mob than prison, had returned and begged to be taken back inside the relative safety of the remaining walls.

After a week the Gordon Riots were over. Chains had been stretched across London streets and troops given the order to stop the riots at all costs. The costs had been high. Hundreds were dead in the streets, hundreds more had died or were injured in the fall of burning buildings. Scores had perished from gulping the fiery rum and brandy that had poured from the overheated barrels of a distillery.

In July, soon after the London streets were quiet again, Sheridan wrote to a friend: "I am at present endeavoring to engage Mrs. Siddons, of the Bath Theatre, which, if I effect, I will inform you." Sarah, pacing the rooms in Paragon Street after the children were asleep, looked out on the tree-dark streets of Bath and argued with herself. London meant more money; Bath was a city of peace. In a thousand years no battle but an occasional duel had been fought in its streets. The ancient walls had never been fortified. Since before Roman times, people had come here to be cured of their pain in the natural mineral springs. Bath was a city of healing, and had been so for her, of healing and challenge. There was, thought Sarah, no better combination. The quiet of London was wary now and tense. Riots could break out again at any moment. Private houses had been burned, not just public buildings, but homes with children sleeping in them. Here her children were safe. She decided to remain in Bath awhile longer.

Sarah continued to gain friends and supporters, and she continued to observe and learn from them how unpredictable people could be. There was the Duchess of Devonshire, beautiful, politically astute, quite unlike what Sarah had supposed a duchess to be. The Reverend Mr. Whalley upset any previous ideas about ministers, since he never ministered to his congregation but hired another cleric to perform his duties while he absorbed the culture of Bath. Generous and kindly, Mr. Whalley enthusiastically tried to live up to the new ideal of the time — the good and sensitive natural man — and reacted with equally tearful fervor to both military bands and the poetry of peace. And there was "Pratty," Samuel Jackson Pratt. He thought of himself as a literary man, and poured out letters to famous people he did not know. A trifle ridiculous, Sarah thought him, watching the deluge of charm he gushed over elderly dowagers whom "others had . . . injured, or neglected." Yet, like most of Bath, she was fond of him and delighted when his play, *The Fair Circassian,* was produced at Drury Lane in 1781.

She realized how different these real people were from the way in which actors of her parents' training would have played them if assigned to characters called The Duchess, The Minister, or The Playwright.

Audiences were delighted with the unexpected in her acting. They saw Mrs. Siddons play characters a dozen other actresses had played before her, but each time they saw a new and individual character. Sarah was aware, too, how much her acting had changed, how much more truth it had. Now she could look back in wonder at her sixteen-year-old self blithely feigning anything from ecstasy to violent death with "correct" gestures and secret glee, and smile, but not indulgently.

In April of 1781, the Siddonses again carried a new baby to Bath Abbey, another daughter, christened Frances Amelia. Unlike their other babies, Frances was weak and sickly. Sarah nursed her with desperate concern, but within a short time the baby died. It was Sarah's first experience with death and it cut deep.

When she again acted a grieving mother she was shocked to feel the lines of the play becoming an expression of her own sorrow, the tears her own as much as the character's. She sensed that her audience was deeply moved and that her playing of the role had a new power and truth. But she came offstage exhausted. It hurt to live her own grief again in the character and let it be so publicly revealed. Yet there was a strange relief in it, too, different from any she could find alone or talking with William. Years later she told a friend that she found acting "a vent for her private sorrows," one which helped her to bear them better. Now she was only beginning to know what this way of working demanded from her, and what it gave back. To act from nature and with truth — neither Garrick nor Henderson had made her understand quite all that meant. The thing must be done to be known.

One evening after a performance of *The Grecian Daughter* a young man presented himself backstage to pay his compliments to Mrs. Siddons. He stared at Sarah with unmasked adoration. "I sketched you once," he said, "in my father's inn at Devizes. I want to paint you now, as the Grecian Daughter."

Startled, Sarah realized the young man was only a boy.

"Thomas Lawrence! Yes, I remember. You brought me luck, I think."

The boy smiled. "Will you come then? I live on Alfred Street. My studio is there."

When she came, Tom Lawrence again did a sketch. He needed a faster, freer medium than oils to carry his own quick, impassioned feeling as he had watched her, in her character, stab the tyrant who oppressed her. The sketch became one of the most famous of the many portraits of Mrs. Siddons.

During the 1781–1782 season, an offer came again from Sheridan. Would Sarah return to Drury Lane? It was, she felt, "a triumphant moment" and, as always, a little frightening. Bath had become home to her. Did she really want London ever again? Yet she needed more challenge, even the challenge of fear again, and she had to think of the children. London would mean more money and that was important with three children to support and a fourth on the way.

She turned to William for advice. London, he assured her, was quieter now. The American Revolution was over; peace would soon be concluded with France. People were tired of war and the government knew it. With peace, all the radicals of different persuasions would settle down. And in London she could earn more money.

News went round Bath quickly that Mrs. Siddons would give her audience "her serious reasons for departure" when she played her farewell performance. After the curtain Sarah reappeared and began reading a poem she had written for the occasion. Midway through she paused, and smiling, moved to the wings where her children waited. With Maria, almost three now, in her arms and Sally and Henry beside her, she returned to the stage:

> *These are the moles that bear me from your side,*
> *Where I was rooted — where I could have died.*
>
> *Have I been hasty? — Am I then to blame?*
> *Answer, all ye who own a parent's name!*

She bowed to the cheering, stamping audience and swiftly left the stage. It was no time for lingering or regrets. London and the future lay ahead.

Chapter Six

In Garrick's Mirror

BY MID-SEPTEMBER of 1782 the playbills at Drury Lane were announcing:

> Mrs. Siddons (From the Theatre Royal, Bath) will shortly make her appearance at this theatre in a Capital Character in Tragedy.

And Mrs. Siddons herself was arguing the problem of just which capital character she would play for her opening.

"But why not Euphrasia?" she demanded. She and William had firmly decided during the rough stage-coach journey to London that she should open with this character from *The Grecian Daughter*. It was a good play, audiences liked her in it, and William thought her excellent in the role.

"No," said Sheridan just as firmly. "Later, perhaps, not now." He looked to his father as he sat, lips pursed and fingers tip to tip, watching Sarah.

"I have it! I have it, Brinsley, just the thing." The old man was gleeful. "Isabella! In *The Fatal Marriage!* And the boy can play young Biron." Off he went in his warm Irish way, listing the advantages, the audience appeal, of Sarah as a beautiful young mother, her son played by her own eight-year-old Harry. Sarah agreed. She knew William would approve the extra fee they might get for Harry's brief appearance.

Privately, Thomas Sheridan told his son that Sarah was at her best in the tender pathos that Isabella demanded. "She fairly melts with grief and love, Brinsley, and that voice! The audience will melt with her, you'll see." So it was decided, and Sarah began studying the part as carefully as if she had never played it before.

The London she came to in 1782 was beautiful with parks and tree-lined squares; houses in the new Georgian design ranged along the streets, the soft shades of their brick and stone set off by the white of shutters and doors. It was a dangerous city, perhaps even more dangerous than when the Siddonses had been here before. Footpads and thugs roamed the streets. On foggy nights, theatregoers hired armed linkboys to carry torches, lighting their way against attack that might strike at any moment from the dark mists.

And still visible were the London poor; not only the jobless urchins whining for tuppence on street corners, but the working poor forced to live in the filth of shaky tenements.

To Tom Holcroft and the radicals the problem was urgent but abstract; the poor must rise and insist upon their rights. To the liberals in Parliament it was a problem that demanded fairness to both sides. To Sarah the poverty of London was human and personal.

The old fears of defeat and failure rose once more. The stench of poverty crawled in her throat and she caught herself swallowing, straining to clear it and succeeding only in rasping her voice. What if she failed this second time? Before, she was young and country audiences were willing to let her try again. Now she was twenty-seven and failure would have no excuse. Had it been a mistake to leave the security of Bath where all her efforts were applauded? She looked forward to her London opening with growing terror.

"Terror" was the word she used in writing to friends. It was no exaggeration. Her future and that of her children would depend on those few hours the evening of October 10, when she would once more step onto the raked boards of Drury Lane and face the judgment of London.

Her tension grew. Suppose they were right, the friends in Bath who worried that her voice might still be too small for Drury Lane, her tones not yet muscular enough to carry the immediacy and power of her feelings? She turned to Thomas Sheridan for reassurance. He knew her work in Bath, he had helped her there; would her voice be all right, did he think?

Sheridan listened and heard the real question underneath: will *I* be all right? He suggested that she play one or two of her scenes for him here in her apartment. She shook her head. She was used to working on her roles late at night, studying and thinking, experimenting with movement but keeping the lines whisper soft so as not to disturb her sleeping children. "Come down to the theatre with me. There alone I can show you exactly what I can do."

Shivering with fever and nervousness, Sarah began the first rehearsal. "I feared to utter a sound above an audible whisper," she wrote later, "but by degrees enthusiasm cheered me into a forgetfulness of my fears, and I unconsciously threw out my voice, which failed not to be heard in the remotest part of the house, by a friend." The friend, of course, was Thomas Sheridan, prowling the dark galleries like a reassuring ghost upon the ramparts.

As the second and third acts progressed, Sarah was puzzled to realize that several of the other actors, whose roles required no tears, were crying. Then, as one scene ended and the company crowded around her applauding, she understood. The rehearsal continued on to her death scene. Suddenly from the wings came a howl of terror. "Mama's dying! I don't want Mama to die!" It was Harry, left to play by himself in one of the dressing rooms, who had wandered back to watch and taken his mother's acting for reality. Comforting him, coaxing him again to laughter, Sarah felt her own nerves continue to tighten.

On the night before second rehearsal, Sarah was unable to sleep, then slept at last too deeply. She was late to rehearsal. It went smoothly, nevertheless, and Tom King, the Shylock to her first dreadful Portia seven years before and now stage manager of Drury Lane, assured her she had nothing to worry about. This time she would be fine on The Night. This was only the eighth, he reminded her, and she had all tomorrow to rest before her opening on the tenth. But no cheering words could reach the core of terror within her. She felt as chill and dismal as the rain that unceasingly drenched the London streets. Reaching home, she tried to greet William and found she could force nothing but a hoarse whisper from her aching throat.

William sent her immediately to bed where she lay stiff and sleepless. Would they have to postpone opening night? She dreaded the thought, longing, as she later wrote, "at least to know the worst." At last she slept and woke next morning to brilliant sunshine pouring in her windows. She began to cry.

William sat down on the bed. "Sally, Sally, what is it? Please don't cry. It's bad for your voice. Look, the sun is out."

"That's why I'm crying! Oh, Sid, I am so thankful." William burst out laughing and noted that at least her voice was better this morning. But Sarah was quite serious in her feeling that sunshine was a good omen, and wrote later: "Even now I am not ashamed of this (as it perhaps may be called) childish superstition. On the morning of the 10th my voice was, most happily, perfectly restored; and again *'The blessed sun shone brightly on me.'*"

Her father arrived that morning to lend his support and found that William needed calming almost more than Sarah. As the hours moved on toward the time they must leave for the theatre, William became ill. By four o'clock it was clear that he must be left, pale and damp-faced, on the sofa, while Roger Kemble conducted his eldest daughter and his first grandson to the theatre.

Roger climbed the steep winding stairs to Sarah's dressing room with her. She had not said a word since leaving home. Now the actor-father knew better than to break her silence with glib words of cheer. He took her icy, shaking hands in his own for a moment, kissed her quickly and left.

Silently she took off her cloak and dress, drew a towel around her shoulders and began to make up. Silently she stood and raised her arms as dressers held out her costume and slipped it over her head, then helped her to pull on the pale silk stockings, buckle her soft leather shoes. In what she would later call a "desperate tranquillity" she forced her concentration away from her own fears, making her mind focus like a burning glass on one thing only — Isabella, the character she was to play.

Outside the theatre carriages were lining up in Drury Lane and Brydges Street. In the lobby excitement was everywhere as the fashionably dressed audience entered, laughing and talking: *My dear, they say she's quite the best actress Bath had seen in years! Ah, but this is London; we shall see. Truly remarkable, the Duchess of Devonshire says.* And they moved on into the house to take their seats in pit and boxes and galleries above. Backstage the callboys were knocking on dressing-room doors with their quick, polite "Beginners, please!"

Sarah took a deep breath and tried to hold her hands steady. It was useless. As a sudden hush from the waiting house penetrated backstage she let her breath out in a wavering sigh. Only minutes remained before she must step out onto the stage where she had repeatedly failed and become in that moment "the sole object of attention to that immense space, lined as it were with human intellect from top to bottom and all around." To a friend she later called it "my fiery trial." Now she knew the moment only as churning terror.

As she stood in the wings, ready for her entrance, someone brought Harry to stand beside her. Only seconds now. The boy looked up, asked a question. She tried to ignore it, to concentrate only on her entrance. And the ghost of a memory whispered, "From Nature, Sarah — ah, come now, give it a roll and a tumble — the natural thing." She bent to answer Harry's question. And the audience of Drury Lane, so long accustomed to the glittering entrances of leading ladies — the entrances that demanded Look at *me!* — saw a young mother enter walking along a street with her son, her head bent toward him, her eyes on his, her steps slowed and shortened in consideration of the little boy.

Scene by scene the play progressed, no longer an old play recited by a new actress but a tragedy happening now at this instant before them. Sarah played as if afire with Isabella's grieving rage and despair. Leaving herself open to the full impact of every moment in the play, saving no shred of energy to spare herself, inhibiting no emotion of her own, Sarah swept the audience with her into tears and unfeigned sobs.

And this was no audience to be easily moved; it was London's most sophisticated. Not merely the fashionable sat in the boxes at Drury Lane this night but the most knowing, the old actors of Garrick's famous days. Thomas Macklin, renowned for his innovations in theatre production and mentor of young David Garrick, listened to the comment of a man beside him that Mrs. Siddons "promises well." Old Macklin snapped, "I think she performs well!" his precise diction underlining the present tense. In another box, London's beloved comedienne and character actress of Garrick's great early company, Kitty Clive, was asked what she thought of Mrs. Siddons' acting. She smiled, her eyes filled with memory, and nodded slowly. "It is all truth and daylight."

By the last act, as Isabella's grief gave way to madness, the audience seemed transported into the action of the play. As her death scene came to an end, they burst into passionate, tumultuous cheering, applauding and shouting until the stage manager wondered if the actors could finish the last brief scenes of the play. No one watching really cared; they knew what happened, they had seen the play before. They had never seen it acted as Mrs. Siddons had just done.

In a daze of exhaustion Sarah left the theatre with her father and Harry. In her own words: "I reached my own quiet fireside . . . half dead; and my joy and thankfulness were of too solemn and overpowering a nature to admit of words, or even tears. My father, my husband, and myself, sat down to a frugal neat supper, in a silence uninterrupted, except by exclamations of gladness from Mr. Siddons. My father enjoyed his refreshments; but occasionally stopped short, and, laying down his knife and fork . . . gave way to tears of happiness."

Sarah woke early the next afternoon, energy renewed, and a little afraid to read the reviews. With daylight, the evening's triumph might prove less real. But William was obviously elated when he handed her the morning papers.

Every critic had poured out his most rapturous words of praise. Her performance had been magnificent, tender, heart-rending. "She wore her sorrows and agonies with such natural simplicity that she arrested all attention." So said the *Morning Chronicle*. The *Morning Post* acclaimed her "the first tragic actress now on the English stage."

Sarah looked up from the paper and touched her nose. "My profile," she said gravely, "is classic! And grand and elegant and striking." William bowed. In an instant she was laughing, then crying. "Sid, it happened! It's real!"

The *Chronicle* spoke for all London in its reaction to Sarah's triumph over her previous failures. "We join in the general joy."

That evening as she started up the stairs to her dressing room, Tom King hailed her. "Wait, Mrs. Siddons. We have moved your things." Puzzled, she followed him to a dressing room on the stage level. It was large and well furnished. Her costumes hung ready, her hairbrush and makeup lay on the table before the huge mirror. She stood unmoving. When she had last been in this room a man's silk robe had lain across the chair, his diamond shoe buckles on the table. "This is David Garrick's dressing room," she said half-angrily.

Tom King nodded. "It will be yours now."

Sarah heard the door shut behind him, and her anger faded. It was foolish, she knew, to resent their not keeping his room for him. It would never bring Davy back to look again into his mirror, his black eyebrows winging upward in amusement. Slowly she raised her head and looked straight into her reflected face. She was twenty-seven now, a woman who had finally learned the lessons Garrick tried to teach the stubborn girl. She moved her fingers along the edge of the glass that had so often mirrored the genius that was David Garrick. Was it only superstition, this "fanciful hope of a little degree of inspiration from it"? He was gone. She was on her own now. And here in his theatre, she would make his gift her own.

Quickly she sat down and began to go through the reviews, looking for the places she had checked, the few comments that pointed out small faults. Tonight she would correct them.

Chapter Seven

Season of Glory

BESIEGED BY LONDON SOCIETY, Sarah wanted to share her success with old friends. She began a habit that would last her lifetime, the writing of notes and letters whenever there was a moment's time, wherever she happened to be.

The day after her opening, in a moment between rehearsal and dining out, she wrote to Mr. Whalley at Bath: "My dear, dear friend, the trying moment is passed, and I am crowned with a success which far exceeds even my hopes. God be praised! I am extremely hurried, being obliged to dine at Linley's; have been at rehearsal of a new tragedy in prose, a most affecting play, in which I have a part I like very much. . . . Oh, how I wished for you last night, to share a joy which was too much for me to bear alone! . . . I am not in perfect possession of myself at present; therefore excuse, my dear Mr. Whalley, the incorrectness of this scrawl, and accept it as the first tribute of love (after the decisive moment) from your ever grateful and truly affectionate, S. Siddons."

London loved theatre; the rise of a new star, especially one as beautiful as the young Mrs. Siddons, was a matter of importance. The "gallery gods" whose cheers or catcalls could determine careers joined the wealthy and fashionable in line outside the Drury Lane box office. The management threw out previously scheduled plays and announced more performances of Mrs. Siddons as Isabella. Every performance sold out.

Brawls and disturbances took place nightly as theatregoers who had been unable to book seats tried to shove their way in through the pit doors. Ladies in rumpled silks and bent hoops were carried out to be revived from fainting fits caused by the commotion. Free-for-all fights occasionally took place between those pushing in and those struggling out.

Newspapers were full of Mrs. Siddons, what she wore, where she went, whom she saw, and how much she earned. Carriages lined the streets outside the theatre after her performances and queued up along The Strand outside her house. Everyone, it seemed, wanted to meet Mrs. Siddons.

At the theatre, Richard Brinsley Sheridan and Tom King spent hours planning the rest of her season. Which parts would she do best in? Which show her beauty and skill to the greatest advantage? And how could they accede to the requests of their more important patrons to cast Mrs. Siddons in this or that favorite play? Sheridan had never struggled so happily with his problems.

Sarah was immersed in the work itself. Later she would look back on these first seasons at Drury Lane as her time of glory. Young, she could give herself unafraid to the exhilaration of success; experienced, she understood the need to choose her own way, to hold the balance steady between public life and private. And if, in these years, her actions now and then nourished the seeds of later trouble, it went unnoticed in "the general joy."

Knowing herself strong and resilient, Sarah gave unstinting energy to the rush of performances, rehearsals, production conferences and costume fittings. Unlike many of her contemporaries, she declined to use her fame as a step to social prominence. She preferred to come home from rehearsals and play with the children for an hour or two before the evening's performance. Blue-eyed Eliza, born a month after Sarah's last performance at Bath, was now almost five months old, and "the most entertaining creature in the world." When she had an evening off, Sarah spent it with William and in the private study of her roles.

And it was true, she admitted when William questioned her, she felt nervous and awkward at big parties where everyone was strange. Onstage, she could be the focus of thousands of eyes and forget them, but as herself — that was a different matter.

Brinsley Sheridan, however, urged her to accept some of the many invitations he knew she was receiving to balls, routs, receptions and suppers. She would, he was sure, enjoy meeting the prominent members of her audience. It was expected of a leading actress in London theatre; she might be thought rude if she constantly declined.

In small gatherings, particularly if the other guests were writers, painters, liberal members of Parliament, Sarah found great enjoyment. The talk challenged her own ideas and opened the restricted life of theatre to the world. But in the midst of larger parties she felt lost. Onstage, every word of her well-rehearsed roles seemed to be improvisation, brilliantly right. As herself, she felt again the uncertain girl she had been years before at Drury, when edged remarks and wit-sharp questions flicked at her. And as she had then, she wished devoutly for a playwright's words with which to answer back. Hiding her shyness, she presented a face of cold, superior dignity. "La!" said an elegant young man, "an affair with Mrs. Siddons? One might as well make love to the Archbishop of Canterbury!" Mrs. Thrale, the friend of Dr. Samuel Johnson, remarked after meeting Sarah at a party, "This is a leaden goddess we are all worshipping. However, we shall soon gild it!" Sarah would never be gilded by London society, but Mrs. Thrale would say when she knew Sarah better and treasured her friendship, "the longer one knows that incomparable creature, the more reasons spring up to esteem and love her."

A Miss Monckton, who belonged to a group of intellectual women called the Blue Stockings, insisted that Sarah accept her invitation to an intimate gathering one Sunday evening. Only three or four friends would be present; they would enjoy having Mrs. Siddons bring her son Harry, and would quite understand if Sarah wished to leave early.

On the appointed evening, Miss Monckton, in towering headdress, a vast display of diamonds, and with two bright spots of rouge on her cheeks greeted Sarah and introduced her to the delighted ladies present. After an hour or so of conversation, Sarah rose to leave — and froze where she stood. From below there came a thunderous pounding on the door, shouts and screams. Miss Monckton smiled. The door crashed open; a crowd of people came pounding up the stairs, shouting to see Mrs. Siddons.

Sarah backed into a chair, pulling Harry close to her. People climbed on chairs and tables to peer over their neighbors' heads at her. Everyone seemed to be jabbing at her with questions. Frantic, Sarah looked from one door to the other. All were jammed solid with excited, shoving "Blues" and their escorts.

A young curate burbled in Sarah's face, "You was adorable last night in Belvidera . . . But then that charming mad scene. . . . Pray, madam, give me leave to ask, was you really in your senses?"

Sarah's fingers rasped across the sticks of her fan. "I strove to do it as well as I could."

Someone pushed the curate aside. "I should be curious to know which part, madam, you yourself esteem the best you play?"

"I shall always endeavor to make that which I am about the best."

A man had just begun talking across Sarah's head to his

companion about the merits and demerits of her acting when an alarmingly fashionable young lady thrust herself through the crowd. "I beg you, Mrs. Siddons, do inform me if you study those enchanting looks and attitudes before a mirror?"

"I never study anything but my author."

"Oh!" the young lady gushed, "then you practice them at rehearsals."

Sarah held tight control on her rising fury. "I seldom rehearse at all!" She jumped to her feet as the crowd parted slightly. It was no use. She was now faced by an apparition in white chiffon and garlanded hair who addressed her as Melpomene, Muse of Tragedy, and proceeded to declaim a poem at her:

> *O thou, whom Nature's goodness calls her own,*
> *Pride of the stage and favorite of the town!*

Harry was howling and Sarah on the verge of joining him when a Mr. Erskine made his way through the mob and escorted her to her carriage. It was two o'clock in the morning.

Throughout October, Sarah played to increasingly enthusiastic audiences. Nevertheless, the opening of her second play, *The Grecian Daughter,* found her as battered by fear as she was by the first. What if the first success were an accident? What if audiences would not accept the physical power, the wild primitive tenderness she believed true of Euphrasia? It would be many years before she could say with amusement, "I well remember my fears and ready tears on each subsequent effort, lest I should fall from my high exaltation."

On opening night she once again withdrew into herself as she dressed and made up, giving no attention to the back-stage turmoil around her. By the time she came onstage she was sensitized, open to each moment as it happened. And when the moment came that she must beg assistance for her old father from the guard, Philotas, and unexpectedly he gave it, she felt herself swept by a transport of gratitude. But there were no lines in the play to express it! Other actresses had let the moment go by. Sarah started toward the guard, her arms outstretched to embrace him, then in one swift motion cast herself in mute gratitude at his feet. There was an instant of utter silence in the great house; then the audience came to its feet in a thousand-voiced gasp. It was acting unlike any they had seen before; they were not even sure it was acting.

The critics expressed their astonishment that Mrs. Siddons could seem so different in this character. She looked taller, her voice had a depth and range quite unlike her Isabella. It was, they decided, a triumph of imagination. Yet as an admiring fellow actor remarked, "She never indulges in imagination at the expense of truth."

At the rival Theatre Royal in Covent Garden, majestic Mrs. Yates read the reviews of Sarah's Euphrasia and began to sputter. "Ridiculous! Crude!" decided Mrs. Yates. Had London audiences forgotten how much they had admired her own studied grace in the part? Given a chance to compare, surely they would come to their senses. Promptly, Mrs.

Yates scheduled a production starring herself in the role. It was a mistake. London greeted her melodious and graceful Euphrasia with a yawn. The lines outside Drury Lane box office lengthened.

However, Mrs. Siddons' triumphant run in the play nearly ended in tragedy. At the climax of it, her part called for her to stab Dionysius, played by John Palmer. She could exert her full strength since the prop dagger was specially built so that the blade slid up into the hilt when it was pushed against anything. One evening as they reached the stabbing scene, Mr. Palmer gazed out over the audience with his usual confident stare. Raising the knife, Sarah plunged it toward his chest. Palmer gave a startled moan and clutched at his side. Sarah jerked her hand away; the dagger clattered to the floor, its unretracted blade covered with blood. She reached toward the writhing Palmer. Her hand, too, was smeared with blood. Fortunately, the thick folds of his costume had deflected the blade and he suffered little more than a grazing cut along his ribs — and the comments of his fellow actors that Palmer had never played so well before.

As her success grew, Sarah worked harder, though her performances seemed quite effortless to her audiences. They thought it a kind of magic the young Mrs. Siddons possessed. But before a scheduled production of *The Tragedy of Jane Shore* her admirers might have seen a tall young woman walking the side streets near Covent Garden and Newgate Prison, her eyes sharp with horror at what she observed. When, as the starving, outcast Jane, Sarah pleaded for help, it was a cry straight from the alleys of London.

When Jane was dying of hunger, barred from the wealthy doors she knocked upon unheard, Sarah disdained to let the character droop exquisitely against the wall, her silken skirts carefully arranged, as other actresses had done. She let her body arch in pain, her face twist in the ugliness of despair. She played the truth of poverty for the rich to see. Her daring was rewarded with acclaim, though it was at times too much for some delicate souls to face. One lady wrote after seeing the play: "Mrs. Siddons ceased to excite pleasure by her appearance, I absolutely thought her the creature perishing from want, 'fainting from loss of food'; shocked at the sight I could not avoid turning from the suffering object." But a child, hearing Jane Shore's exhausted whisper that she was starving, leaned from a nearby box and cried out, "Madam! Madam! Do take my orange, please!"

Coming offstage one night, Sarah caught sight of herself in Garrick's mirror and burst into laughter. Still in Jane's character, her reflected face seemed gaunt, the lines etched forever. And suddenly she had thought of that long-ago day at Guy's Cliffe when, her face glowing with health, she had churned her hair into disarray and declaimed Jane's woe with all the élan of total ignorance. No wonder poor David Garrick had turned away to the window. What a miracle of control he'd been not to have doubled up in whoops of laughter!

December came and with it time for Sarah's first benefit. It was to be a brilliant occasion. London was alive with Christmas spirit, a counterpoint of caroling bells and begging urchins. Holly and ivy draped the stage door entrance, and William Siddons' bank account was already a hundred pounds richer from a gift presented to Sarah by a barristers' club.

She met with Sheridan to choose her benefit play. *Venice Preserved* would be right, he thought. Sarah was delighted. Though she would never say it to Sheridan, the play felt lucky to her. It was in *Venice Preserved* that Lord Bruce and Henrietta Boyle had seen her that evening in Cheltenham — seven years ago!

"I quite agree, Mr. Sheridan," she said, "and I am sure it will meet with Mr. Siddons' approval." She wished she felt as easy with young Sheridan as with his father, but she was always too aware that she stood before England's most brilliant wit and caught herself being defensive in case he might be laughing at her.

Sheridan bowed slightly. "I'm certain Mr. Siddons will be pleased to hear that the management will dispense with the usual arrangement of retaining the take from six boxes for its own fee and will allow Mrs. Siddons the entire amount." He smiled. "A small Christmas gift."

Sarah blinked. That would mean at least another hundred pounds. Was he serious? "I — we — are most grateful."

"The gratitude is mine. Your performances have brought new health to Drury Lane's box office."

Sarah stared at him, hurt and disappointed. Was that all her work meant to Sheridan? Was that all his theatre meant to him, just money? But what did he spend it on? Certainly not the theatre; Tom King could never get enough for costumes and scenery. There were rumors that Sheridan was constantly in trouble with his creditors. She was suddenly aware of silence stretching out and found herself blurting, "Is that what your theatre means to you, Mr. Sheridan, just a box office?"

"Of course! You've heard them, haven't you, Mrs. Siddons, whispering behind their fans and snuffboxes, 'Sheridan's favorite payday is tomorrow,' and 'Sheridan always has his hand in the till at Drury Lane'?" He began to move about his office, from desk to window and back again, past the costume sketches on the wall. "Well, why not? From what other till than that of my own theatre should I draw? From the public funds? From the taxes paid by the poor on the gin that alone makes life bearable for them? Or from a sinecure offered by our plump little King to buy my vote in Parliament?"

Sarah sat motionless, stunned by the passionate thrust of his voice. Sheridan faced her. "Do you know, Mrs. Siddons, what it costs a man to run for election and maintain himself in Parliament?" She shook her head. "Enough to bar most men from trying — unless they have inherited wealth or can be bought. I pay my own costs and vote my own way." He moved to the window. "Look there, at London. Our rivers are polluted with filth. Robbery and murder roam our streets, and the streets stink with poverty. Our very bread is contaminated with plaster and crumbled shells to make it whiter — and more profitable. Men, and women too, are thrown into prison for debts of a few shillings or the theft of some rotten meat; and they die from jail fever before they can be heard. Landlords collect their profits while the buildings they leave unrepaired collapse and crush the occupants — never the rich, of course. The poor suffer most, Mrs. Siddons, and poor men have little representation in our Parliament."

Sheridan leaned against the edge of his desk and flicked a speck of snuff from his soft green waistcoat. "I have proved, Mrs. Siddons, that a man of lowly birth, a player's son, can attain Parliament." He tossed a gold coin in the air and caught it neatly. "And I thank the Drury Lane box office for the honor."

Sarah stared at him. This was Richard Brinsley Sheridan, author of the most brilliant comedies in a generation, *The Rivals* and *The School for Scandal?* She thought again of Garrick, insisting that one must always look for the touch of comedy within the tragic, the serious thread under the flow of laughter.

"Mr. Sheridan, I . . ."

Quickly he rose. "Forgive me, Mrs. Siddons, I bore you."

"No!"

For a moment there was neither movement nor speech between them, then Sheridan spoke softly. "Poor men made a revolution in America. . . ."

"Surely not here? The peace has been signed. Surely, revolution is past?"

"Oh, is it?" Sheridan whirled to face her. "Is it now? Have you read Tom Paine, Mrs. Siddons? His *Common Sense?*"

"No, I haven't."

"Do so! Tom Paine was an Englishman, his ideas born here, out of English life. And France stirs, even now." A

Richard Brinsley Sheridan. Engraving after a portrait by Sir Joshua Reynolds. (From the Raymond Mander and Joe Mitchenson Theatre Collection)

gleeful smile lit Sheridan's face. "There is a play — by Beaumarchais — that's causing quite a noise, though Louis of France refuses to allow its public performance. Tom Holcroft may do a translation in English."

"Tom Holcroft? He was in my father's company."

Sheridan nodded. "A dangerous man, Mrs. Siddons, and a dangerous play, the *Marriage of Figaro!* It laughs at the precious world of King Louis and Farmer George."

Sarah laughed. It was as true as everyone said, Brinsley Sheridan had indestructible charm. "Will you produce it?"

He shrugged. "Who can tell? It may depend on the box office of Drury Lane."

Sheridan had no need to worry. Crowds literally fought for tickets to Mrs. Siddons' benefit and William received more than eight hundred pounds to bank, invest or spend as he chose. Sarah was grateful that William was a cautious man and managed her earnings well. There were times one could be glad of a husband who lacked dash and daring.

Once more, in *Venice Preserved,* Sarah introduced a new interpretation of a traditional role. Studying the scene in which the tormented Belvidera goes mad, she paused. Why this custom that all mad heroines must waft about in white satin? Ridiculous. She threw the fluttery white gown aside and put on dark robes, a dark cloak flung over her shoulders. And a critic noted: "The distraction which conducts her to her end was without its eternal white satin dress, and then only did the action upon the ground, 'I'll dig, dig the den up,' appear more than noisy vehemence." It was also noted that never before had Mr. Brereton played so ardently as he did with Mrs. Siddons. Backstage, the actors smirked at each other and muttered that Brereton was certainly head over heels, even if he was a married man. Sarah ignored the talk and tried to ignore Mr. Brereton except onstage.

Late in December, Sheridan knocked on her dressing room door and greeted her with a wicked grin. "Dear Mrs. Siddons, I have the honor to inform you that in spite of my odious politics, His Majesty, George the Third, has commanded a performance by Mrs. Siddons in *The Grecian Daughter* for January 2, 1783!"

It was a gala night with jewels and silks shining in the mellow candlelight. Their Majesties were enchanted by the new actress. So much so, that deplorable as they found Sheridan's political bent, they returned on four subsequent nights in January to be sure of seeing Mrs. Siddons in all her roles. The Queen, however, found some of the portrayals so moving that she had to turn her back to the stage. She could not bear to watch such realistic suffering.

In the spring an elaborate carriage drew up before number 149 The Strand. It bore the Royal Arms on the side and footmen alighted to hand Mrs. Siddons inside. Sarah was on her way to give a Reading to the King and Queen. She wished nervously that William had been invited. Now she must somehow get through it alone, knowing nothing of Court etiquette and dressed in a most elaborate and difficult gown. Disgusted, Sarah peered down over the triple row of ruffles, extremely wide hoops and very long, saque-back dress that Court custom required. If she had to step backward, she would certainly trip on this skirt!

Arriving in the anteroom, Sarah waited for her summons into the Queen's chambers. There was a flurry at the door and the King ambled in pulling a wicker go-cart in which the three-year-old Princess Amelia rode. As the King moved off to chat with someone across the room, the Princess climbed out of her cart and immediately trotted to Sarah.

"She is adorable!" Sarah said to a lady-in-waiting. "Oh, I should like to kiss her," and forgetting royal privilege in her genuine love of children, she bent to do so. Pulling back, the Princess drew herself up haughtily and extended her hand. With a slight gulp, Sarah regained her dignity, and leaning precariously forward, raised the child's hand to her lips.

At last Queen Charlotte was ready and the Reading began. After a few scenes from Milton and Shakespeare, the Queen suggested that perhaps Mrs. Siddons would care to rest for a few moments and take some refreshments in the adjoining room. Sarah was about to say a thankful yes when she remembered her gown and the long saque-train draped behind her on the slickly polished floor. One must back from the presence of royalty, she knew. But how — without falling flat? "Thank you, Your Majesty, I am quite refreshed," said Sarah and proceeded quickly into the next selection. Several times the worried Queen put the same suggestion to her and each time Sarah smiled and declined.

When the Reading was over and the King and Queen had left the room, Sarah fled to the waiting carriage on trembling legs and aching arches. Their Majesties clucked to each other with amazement that evening on the subject of

Mrs. Siddons' physical endurance — astonishing for such a fragile-appearing young woman!

On June 5, the last night of the 1782–1783 season, Sarah once again played Isabella to thundering applause. As she packed her makeup and costumes away, she was unconscious of any backstage bitterness toward her or "the Kemble clan." But it was there, simmering beneath the prosperous surface of Drury Lane. Sarah had persuaded Sheridan to hire both Frances and Elizabeth Kemble, although neither was a more than adequate actress, and it was almost certain that her brother John Philip would be engaged for the fall season. Already, in the men's dressing rooms the actors were beginning to mutter angrily that John Philip Kemble would have no easy time of it, by God, if he tried to take their roles from them. Never mind if his sister Sarah Kemble Siddons were queen of the London stage.

Chapter Eight

All Truth and Daylight

RICHARD DALY, actor-manager of the Smock Alley Theatre in Dublin, had offered Sarah a summer tour of Ireland. William considered the terms excellent and Sarah was elated. She had never seen Ireland and never been to sea. It would be an adventure. John Philip and Elizabeth Inchbald would join them in Dublin and together with the Breretons they would all make up a company.

Costumes packed and children off to the country, Sarah and William left London four days after her season there had closed. By post chaise they traveled to Holyhead, Wales, where they would take a ship for the sea journey to Dublin. Embarking from Holyhead, Sarah was filled with excitement. She stood at the ship's rail with William, inhaling great draughts of the salty air, exulting in the sweep of sky and wind and endless moving water. As the sails filled and the ship moved beyond sight of land, Sarah whispered to William, "Good God! How tremendous! How wonderful!"

"You're not afraid?"

"Awed, but not terrified." She laughed. "A pleasing terror. I feel myself in the hands of a great and powerful God 'whose mercy is over all His works.'" She braced herself against the swiftly accelerating roll and pitch of the deck.

A short while later her joy had turned to queasiness. She was inelegantly and thoroughly seasick. In a letter to Mr. Whalley, she suggested the remedy: "My dear friend, let me give you a little wholesome advice; allways (you see I have forgot to spell) go to bed the instant you go on board, for by lying horizontally, and keeping very quiet, you cheat the sea of half its influence."

Sarah felt their welcome to Dublin something less than a triumph. Arriving after midnight, the actors were ushered into a tiny, bare-walled customs office Sarah labeled "a dungeon" where they sat for nearly two hours. At last, their costumes crammed back into trunks, they were let out to wander through the rain-lashed streets in search of lodgings.

At every door they tried, the response was the same. A nightcapped landlady would peer suspiciously at the sodden group and exclaim, "I'll not be takin' in ladies — if that's what ye are — at this time of the night!" and slam the door. Only after long argument did Mr. Brereton finally get them beds at the lodging house where his father stayed.

Lines formed early for Sarah's first performance. Dublin

was eager to see London's newest star and curious to watch her act with her brother. John Philip and Sarah had not acted together since their York circuit days and their pleasure was echoed in racketing applause.

The Irish approved John Philip Kemble. He had been in their country for two years, and he could answer yes to the question asked all men of honor in Ireland: "Had he ever *blazed?*" He had. There had been a quarrel with one of his managers. In the ensuing duel neither man had been seriously injured but John Philip's honor was secure. His vast dignity onstage and equal gift for carousing off intrigued the Irish. They were not so sure they liked Sarah. Doubtless a great actress, they said, but surely a bit standoffish.

Sarah was no happier with the Irish. The rowdy houses of Dublin and Cork reminded her of the huge parties she hated. Spectators might bound onto the stage and jostle the actors. She could expect to be greeted halfway through a tragic speech by an alcoholic howl from the pit, "Ah, Sally, me jewel, how are ye?" and felt lucky if the questioner refrained from leaping onto the stage and embracing her. Richard Daly, the vain, unscrupulous manager, and the frequently drunk Mr. Digges, the character actor, made life even more difficult for Sarah.

Snide comments about her began appearing in the papers. One article, presumably written by Digges, was so hilarious in its insults that reprints gained circulation in England, particularly among actors who felt threatened by the Kembles. At the theatre in Smock Alley, said the article, Mrs. Siddons' acting moved her audience so deeply that "several fainted, even before the curtain drew up! . . . The very fiddlers in the orchestra blubbered like children crying for their bread and butter; and when the bell rang for music between the acts, the tears ran from the bassoon player's eyes in such plentiful showers that they choked the finger stops, making a spout of the instrument. . . . The briny pond in the pit was three feet deep. . . . True it is that Mr. Garrick never could make anything of her, and pronounced her below mediocrity. . . . But what of that?"

Sarah might have found the article as funny as others did but for those last remarks. To have the old failure dragged up again hurt deeply. Had she struck back with a wit-sharp blast or let her occasionally wild temper explode, the Irish would undoubtedly have cheered, and she herself felt better. She was a stranger in a country she failed to understand and she maintained an outward coolness. She confided her real feelings to the Whalleys in a letter filled with scathing descriptions of Ireland and the Irish. The letter was at first undelivered, then returned to her at her London address. It had been opened in Ireland. Sarah blithely noted to the Whalleys: "For God's sake, my dear friends, pray for my memory. . . . I must never show my face there again." Had she taken her own words more seriously she might have spared herself future trouble. Sarah's season in Ireland had been profitable, however, and the Siddonses returned to London two thousand pounds richer. Two Irish charities had been aided by benefits Sarah had performed for them, and on the whole her Irish summer seemed worth the trouble.

Home again, Sarah's fall season began brilliantly, with a

Command Performance requested by the King and Queen to welcome their dear Mrs. Siddons back to London. Preparing for her entrance, Sarah stole a glimpse of the royal entourage from the wings. How strange, she thought, those two homely, pleasant people in all that grandeur! Can the King, sitting there in his plain suit of Quaker-dark clothes, be ignorant of the foulness and corruption of his city, the poverty of so many of his people? Yet how could he know when even here in a public theatre he was isolated by the splendor surrounding him? Beside him in the crimson and gold velvet-draped box sat the Queen, a white satin dumpling in a diamond headdress. To their left in a canopied blue and silver box lounged their eldest son, the Prince of Wales, wearing a blue velvet suit with gold lace at his wrists and throat. Could these people ever understand why hungry men revolted? She sighed and wished the Queen had not turned away from Jane Shore's agony. Silently then, Sarah made way for a stagehand dragging a wing of scenery into place and withdrew into her character of Isabella.

On September 30, Sarah went through the torments of opening night nerves for John Philip, now under contract to Drury Lane. With William and the Sheridans she watched her brother, strikingly handsome and graceful, play Hamlet. It was a studied, careful and sensitive portrayal. London critics gave their approval though they looked in vain for the impassioned feeling of his sister's playing. John was an imposing figure on the stage, so tall and strong that Sir Walter Scott once said he was built "on a scale suitable for the stage, and almost too large for a private apartment."

Sarah wished that Elizabeth Inchbald, now a successful playwright, and John Henderson would move from Covent Garden and join her and John Philip at Drury. Henderson shook his head. There was no room for him in the same company with John Philip; they played the same line of parts. Mrs. Inchbald, for several years a widow and more than half in love with Sarah's tall brother, said, "N-no, dear heart. The t-two of you would never p-play in my comedies, and without you, a play has no chance at D-drury Lane."

Many of the regular Drury company chafed with resentment. The Siddons-Kemble clan was taking over the theatre, they grumbled. Frances and Elizabeth Kemble were not good actresses, yet they were getting parts. John Philip was a starchy fellow and one to keep an eye on, mind you, or he'd have all Mr. Brereton's and Mr. Palmer's parts and be running Sheridan's theatre for him if Brinsley didn't watch out.

Brinsley Sheridan kept his ears deaf to the muttering. Mrs. Siddons was packing the house; if she wished her family with her, let her have them. He had troubles enough in Parliament. How would the English government turn if revolution spread to France? Would it mean war again and rising prices on poor men's bread? What could he do, if so? Thoughtfully, Sheridan stroked on his pale leather gloves and snapped his walking stick under his arm. With practiced charm he doffed his hat to a waiting creditor and strode out the door, humming a song from *The Beggar's Opera*. Let the Drury actors complain. Mrs. Siddons was queen of the London stage and a handsomer girl than England's own.

Queen Charlotte, round cheeks pink with earnest concern for her daughters, appointed Sarah Reading Preceptress to the Royal Princesses that they might be certain to speak English correctly in spite of their Germanic background. "The position, I daresay, is little in demand," Sarah remarked to William, "since it is one of all honor, I believe, and no salary."

She was pleased, however, and truly grateful when the Queen appointed her son Henry to one of England's finest schools, the Charterhouse. She and William alone could never have afforded the boy such an opportunity. And Sarah nodded sweetly and agreed to be careful when the King, with paternal fussiness, warned her against the use of white powder on the neck as being detrimental to the health.

Far more than her visits with royalty Sarah was enjoying her increasing acquaintance with painters and playwrights, young novelists and essayists. Most of them, like Sheridan, were liberals. Some, like Tom Holcroft, were outright radicals determined to remake the world. All were certain life would be better if ordinary men could have liberty and equality. Sarah, sympathetic with Holcroft's struggles, introduced him to the Duchess of Devonshire in the hope that the Duchess might help Holcroft as she had Sheridan.

Making up before her mirror one evening, Sarah looked with disgust at her elaborate, tormented hair style and the box of reddish-gold powder. Both conformed to the usual stage practice. And both, she thought, belonged to a world that was passing. Holcroft and the other young writers said that in Europe young people were rebelling against false fashions, wearing their hair loose and free of powder. With a smile she remembered the tales of Peg Woffington's cry, "Let Liberty reign!" And truth and nature, Sarah added to herself. Suddenly hairpins and ribbons were flying, powder was tossed into a bottom drawer. Sarah went onstage that night with her hair unpowdered and shining, curved close around her head in thick braids.

Sir Joshua Reynolds, England's Principal Painter to the King, rushed backstage after the performance to congratulate her. His painter's eye was filled with delight to see the true shape of a woman's head, far more beautiful, he said, than the traditional custom of kneading and lathering hair, powder, and pomade into a mass of curls like small cannon all over the head! Sir Joshua mentioned that he had seen Thomas Lawrence's portrait of her as the Mourning Bride and found it most interesting. He had been thinking of Mrs. Siddons as the Muse of Tragedy. Would she sit for him?

Encouraged by his response to her experiment with hairdressing, Sarah arrived for her sitting without hoops, letting the skirt of her simple dark gown fall freely from the waist. Sir Joshua beamed approval. Indicating the carved chair he had placed on a dais, he bowed. "Ascend your undisputed throne!" As he began adjusting his canvas, Sarah turned her head slightly to look at one of his paintings. Sir Joshua was elated. The very pose!

When he had finished the portrait of *Mrs. Siddons as the Tragic Muse,* Sarah inspected it carefully, fascinated by the blends of color, the movement of light and shadow, learning as always from another artist's work. She bent to examine a

*Mrs. Siddons as the Tragic Muse. Engraving after
a portrait by Sir Joshua Reynolds.
(From the Raymond Mander
and Joe Mitchenson Theatre Collection)*

Mrs. Siddons. Engraving after the portrait by Sir Thomas Gainsborough. (From the Raymond Mander and Joe Mitchenson Theatre Collection)

scribble of gold in the lower corner: *Joshua Reynolds Pinxit 1784.* The famous painter nodded. "I cannot lose the opportunity afforded me of going down to posterity on the hem of your garment."

Thomas Gainsborough, who painted Sarah in 1785, was less gallant. After struggling for some time, he flung his brush aside and snapped, "Dammit, madam, there is no end to your nose!" It was something Sarah had often thought, but ill at ease in the rich velvet gown and feathered hat Gainsborough insisted on, she was too shy to tell him so. She guessed, however, what others would clearly see: Gainsborough was too enamored of his own talents to see an actress or her profession with the warm understanding of Reynolds or Lawrence.

The season of 1783–1784 continued with the brilliance of its beginning. And Sarah worked harder than ever. Challenging herself, she played Isabella in Shakespeare's *Measure for Measure,* a cold and priggish character, and made her somehow sympathetic. In the traditional glitter of a Royal Command night for Shakespeare's *King John,* Sarah defied tradition, left her hoops on the dressing-room floor and robed her character in flowing black with "a train of satin, and a petticoat of white," her hair disheveled and wild. The audience loved it. They understood that here was an actress of passion and intellect who must "be herself alone."

Tired of queens and great ladies of the past, Sarah decided to play Mrs. Beverly in *The Gamester,* a contemporary Englishwoman beggared and destroyed by her husband's obsession with the favorite vice of the time, gambling. There would be scarcely a woman in the audience who could not identify with Mrs. Beverly.

John Philip was delighted to play Mr. Beverly, but William was uncertain about Sarah's choice. She was successful in her great roles, he cautioned, why change? But Sarah's audiences found it one of her most exciting roles. Every moment she played seemed to happen for the first time, right now before them. Her pantomime and movement seemed totally impulsive. At the end of the play, when she knelt beside her dead husband in his bare prison room, her eyes fixed blankly on his face, "the powers of life seemed suspended in her," wrote an admiring fellow actor. "Her sister and Lewson gently raised her, and slowly led her unresisting from the body, her gaze never for an instant averted from it; when they reached the prison door she stopped, as if awakened from a trance, with a shriek of agony . . . and rushing from them, flung herself as if for union in death, on the prostrate form before her."

Sarah never merely pretended the break from her sister and Lewson, or the rush to her husband's body. A new actor in the part of Lewson had to be warned to brace himself; Sarah threw her whole physical energy into the breakaway, and an actor not forewarned might find himself knocked flat. This tremendous expenditure of energy exhausted Sarah, and she sometimes fainted for a moment after the curtain came down, but it was this complete giving of herself that swept audiences along with her. Neither those watching nor those playing with her could hold themselves apart from the impassioned thrust of her playing.

Sarah now fully understood her own method of work and knew that if she would act with the truth that had so moved old Kitty Clive, she could not spare herself in any way. When she played Constance in *King John,* she faced the problem of a character who was offstage during the very scenes which were supposed to arouse the tremendous emotional state in which she must enter. Other actresses who attempted the part relied on a few hasty moments to get in the mood for this entrance, launched themselves onstage, and hoped for the best. Sarah left her dressing-room door open so that she could hear and live through every cruel event her character must react to. She listened to the "sickening sounds" of the military march that caused "bitter tears of rage, disappointment, betrayed confidence . . . to gush into my eyes." And when she finally came onstage, audiences were overwhelmed by the force of her emotion.

She demanded of herself an intense power of concentration on the events of the play, until this concentration, "co-operating also with a high degree of enthusiasm, *shall have transfused the mind of the actress into the person and situation"* of the character. The result, according to an actor who had worked with her, was that the spectator was completely carried along with her and *"wept when she wept, smiled when she smiled, and each motion of her heart became in turn his own."*

Chapter Nine

To Dublin and Back

FOR SOME TIME, Sarah's friends had been suggesting that she must meet Dr. Samuel Johnson, London's dominant literary figure. Johnson's friends had been putting the same idea to him. Neither looked with enthusiasm on the idea. Why, snorted Johnson, should he want to meet "that jade, Siddons"? Sarah confessed to John Philip that she was nervous about talking to anyone who had written *A Dictionary of the English Language*. John, who often visited Dr. Johnson, promised to accompany her. On the way there he described the writer, crippled from gout, heavy with age, his large head often jerking and trembling from attacks of palsy. John knew he must tap Sarah's unfailing warmth toward those who suffered before she could lose her shyness in the face of Johnson's reputation for bluntly delivered and often rude opinions.

They entered a room apparently furnished with books and little else. Even the chairs were hidden under piles of books and manuscripts. Lumbering painfully to his feet, Dr. Johnson bowed to Sarah. "Madam, you who so often occasion a want of seats to other people, will the more readily excuse the want of one yourself." A chair was soon cleared for Sarah and within a few minutes she was completely captivated by Johnson's good-humored discussion of English drama. He asked what character interested her most. After a moment's thought Sarah mentioned Queen Katherine in Shakespeare's *Henry the Eighth*. "Madam," said Johnson, "whenever you perform it, I will once more hobble out to the theatre myself." He explained that he no longer attended the theatre, being too nearly blind to see except from a place close to the stage, yet he hated to sit in so conspicuous a spot. Gently, Sarah proposed that she could have a comfortable chair placed in the wings where he could watch the play unobserved.

Soon they spoke of David Garrick and the old man's rumbling voice was proud. "Garrick, Madam, was no declaimer . . . he was the only actor I ever saw, whom I could call a master both in tragedy and comedy. . . . A true conception of character, and the natural expression of it, were his excellencies." Then, revealing his own self-consciousness at social occasions as much as his admiration for the younger man, he added, "And after all, Madam, I thought him less to be envied on the stage than at the head of a table."

The visit passed pleasantly for both. "Neither praise nor money, the two powerful corrupters of mankind, seem to have depraved her," wrote Dr. Johnson to his friend, Mrs. Thrale. "I shall be glad to see her again." Sarah returned for many more visits and Dr. Johnson always conducted her to the head of the stairs where, bowing, he said, "Dear Madam, I am your most humble servant." To the regret of both, he was never again well enough to attend the theatre and see "that jade, Siddons" act for him.

Genius now became the word constantly used about Sarah in reviews, in letters to the papers, in drawing-room conversations. London's other leading actresses found the word grating against their egos. To Mrs. Crawford it was particularly annoying. She was, after all, a veteran actress. She had drawn houses as large as Sarah's in Dublin the summer before, and she was only too pleased when her friends began writing heated letters to the daily papers praising her merits and damning Mrs. Siddons' faults. The rivalry extended to their leading men now that Sarah's brother often played opposite her. Said the news paragraphs, Mr. Henderson of Covent Garden was warm, human, played "from Nature," while Mr. Kemble was cold, solemn and intellectual. London was moving fast toward theatrical battle.

At first Sarah held back. She knew that any competition between her and Mrs. Crawford must be in a leading role, yet Mrs. Crawford was aging rapidly. Theatre child that she was, Sarah knew all actors, however great, must one day confront the evidence that their voices could no longer carry the power of their feelings, their bodies no longer sustain the physical demands of acting, and that younger actors must take over their famous roles. It was bitter knowledge for an actor to reach, and Sarah had no wish to force it upon Mrs. Crawford. But when the papers announced that Mrs. Crawford was shortly to "attack" Mrs. Siddons, and to her surprise Sarah read that she had "declared to stand the conflict" she recognized the inevitable.

The Theatre Royal in Covent Garden announced that Mrs. Crawford would appear in the role she had made famous, Lady Randolph in the tragedy *Douglas*. A difficult, emotionally demanding part, Mrs. Crawford had made it her own so thoroughly that any other actress attempting it knew she would be compared line for line and move for move with the famous Irish actress. Drury Lane announced Sarah would play the role. It was open challenge and London knew it. Gleefully the bets were laid.

Covent Garden was packed for Mrs. Crawford's performance. She played the part in the grand manner, her skirts held wide with hoops, her hair powdered and fashionably coiffed. In the noted scene where a fisherman tells Lady Randolph that years before he had rescued the baby son she thought drowned, Mrs. Crawford as usual leaped at the man with a wild screech of hope, "Was he alive?" She received her usual applause. But many were shocked to note how she had aged, how "harsh and discordant" her voice had become, though still "she produced abundant tears."

A short time later, Drury Lane was equally packed. Dressed in a simple black gown that flowed with her body as she moved, her hair unpowdered, Sarah worked with total forgetfulness of competition. She played Lady Randolph as she understood her. Yet when the fisherman's scene began, the audience waited in tense expectancy. Could Mrs. Siddons outshriek her rival? The fisherman gave his speech. There was a second's pause as Sarah stood unmoving. Then her voice came in a painful whisper, "Was he alive?" Those present later said they could actually feel the shiver that went through the great house in response to the stripped reality of the line. "He was," answered the fisherman. Mistaking his meaning, Sarah turned on him in unleashed agony:

> *Inhuman that thou art!*
> *How couldst thou kill what waves and tempests spared?*

The night was a triumph Mrs. Crawford never forgave; five years later she was to join with Mrs. Yates in a campaign of venomous gossip about Sarah.

Another triumphant London season over, Sarah left for a tour of Scotland, then Ireland. She had never played in the north and was unprepared for the reserve of the Edinburgh audiences. On opening night she played her first scenes to complete silence; where she was accustomed to applause at the end of scenes there was not a murmur of reaction. As the play progressed the silence continued. Were they playing to stones? When her next scene came, Sarah threw every ounce of energy into it, hurling the lines to a dramatic climax. Suddenly a man's voice from the gallery remarked judicially, "That's no' bad!" The house burst into peals of laughter and then applause. Sarah had won even the reserved Scots, and before she left Edinburgh she was given a silver tea service inscribed, "As a mark of esteem for superior genius and unrivalled talents. . . ."

Sarah and William left for the village of Portpatrick where they would set sail for Ireland. The minister there, Dr. Mackenzie, was most curious about how Mrs. Siddons could produce tears onstage. Straight-faced, William explained, "Small beer is good for crying. The day my wife drinks small beer, she cries amazingly; she is really pitiful. But if I was to give her porter, or any stronger liquor, she would not be worth a farthing."

The Reverend Doctor was also taken aback by Sarah's reaction to the wild Scottish shore from which the Siddonses were embarking. She turned to look at the sea churning against the jutting rocks, the craggy hills rising behind them, and uttered "all at once one of her wild cries. . . . It was melancholy, and was mournful, and was piercingly loud." It also brought the natives rushing from their cottages. Said Dr. Mackenzie, "Such a scene I have never witnessed."

William was unmoved. He took Sarah by the arm. "Come, my dear, what is all this for? You don't propose to swim to Ireland — Egad, if you don't make haste, the vessel will sail absolutely."

Trouble began almost immediately in Ireland. Daly, still manager of the Smock Alley Theatre, had accustomed himself to take center stage no matter how small his role or how unimportant he was in a scene. Sarah found herself trying to play a crucial scene in the shadows at one side while Daly preened center in the light. Calmly she suggested a change in their positions. Grudgingly, Daly agreed, but he never forgave her.

Malicious rumors and accusations began to appear in the

papers. Most were letters from correspondents who, in the custom of the time, signed themselves "Justinian," "Brutus," or some other classic name which disguised their identities. People were openly guessing the letters were inspired, if not actually written, by Daly and his friends. No one could prove it. The Siddonses were helpless to refute the lies of nameless accusers.

When she became briefly though seriously ill, Sarah was accused of feigning in order to avoid her acting commitments. If, tired from illness, she declined the barrage of requests for her appearance at parties, balls and benefits, paragraphs noted "facts" about her coldness and inhumanity. It was noted that she was willing to stay with the O'Neils of Shane's Castle in great luxury and the implication of snobbery was clear. No one bothered to note that Mrs. O'Neil was the former Henrietta Boyle, who had been Sarah's friend since that long-ago summer in Cheltenham when she had supervised Sarah's wardrobe.

When William, starved for work of his own, decided to assume full responsibility for Sarah's affairs, he precipitated the worst of her Irish troubles. Mr. Digges arrived at rehearsal one day with apparently a worse hangover than usual. A short while later he collapsed. A doctor was summoned, rehearsal dismissed, and later that day came news that Mr. Digges had suffered a stroke. Daly immediately approached William with a request that Sarah play a benefit for the stricken actor. William, still angry at the treatment Sarah had received from Daly and Digges, and concerned for her health, refused. It was impossible, he said; they were leaving almost immediately to fulfill Sarah's engagements in other cities, and she had already agreed to give a benefit for the men in Marshalsea Prison.

Sarah was nevertheless disturbed. Digges was old, he would probably never act again. Why not, she suggested, do a benefit after her regular season was over? William agreed. Daly consented to open his theatre for the night, but he had already talked widely of Mrs. Siddons' refusal to play for poor, distressed Digges. There was a renewed burst of paragraphs in the Dublin papers flaying Sarah for coldness and inhumanity.

When the scheduled season closed, Sarah began trying to assemble a cast for Mr. Digges's benefit. Most of the actors had unconcernedly left on holiday. When she was able to assemble a company they were all strangers to her. None had time for a rehearsal. Somehow the show got on, though with her disciplined attitude toward theatre, Sarah felt it a scene of "disgust and confusion." Since the benefit realized a large sum for Mr. Digges, she noted: "I put my disgust in my pocket, since money passed into his." With a sense of deep relief she left Ireland and headed for the peace of London and their new home in Gower Street.

After cautious thought, William had decided that their finances warranted a home of their own. He leased a small house at 14 Gower Street. The back of it opened into the gardens of Bedford Square, with trees and flowers, an archery range, and paths across open fields where Sarah and the children could walk to Highgate or Hampstead. The best of city and country she thought it, and happily singing, "Oranges and lemons say the bells of Saint Clement's," she installed furniture, books and children in their new home.

Sarah's happiness was short-lived. She was hardly settled in when worried friends began arriving at Gower Street. Had Sarah heard? Did William know? What were they going to do? Clippings and newspapers piled up in the Siddonses' living room. The summer crop of venom from Ireland had been transplanted to England. Now there was more: the "incomparable genius" had become "Lady Sarah Save-All" and other snide nicknames. Actors, it was said, knew that Sarah avoided the collections for indigent fellow players. Another story had it that she lingered after the service in church to avoid the collection plate. Vicious cartoons appeared. Sarah's Irish troubles were the opportunity the anti-Siddons-Kemble faction had been waiting for.

There were now stories that Sarah had not only refused to play for Mr. Digges's benefit but also for her fellow actor Mr. Brereton unless he paid her fifty pounds. The truth was that Sarah and Brereton had agreed to play in each other's benefits for the thirty-pound fee usual between leading actors. Each had been ill at the time of the other's benefit and had not played. After Brereton was ill, Sarah had offered to play for him for twenty pounds. When he could not arrange a suitable date she had offered him a cash payment to help make up what he would lose.

Frantically William dashed about London protesting to anyone who would listen that Sarah had played four benefits in addition to one for Digges: two for Irish charities and two for fellow actors, Mr. Lewes and Mr. Aiken. William wrote to Digges asking him now that he was better to write a letter clearing Sarah. He asked Brereton to do the same. And he wrote an earnest, awkward letter of his own to the papers.

Sheridan was reassuring. He had announced that Mrs. Siddons would open her season on October 5 with John Philip Kemble in *The Gamester*. Tickets were going well. She must not be fearful; there were, he insisted, letters defending her as well as denouncing her.

On the morning of October 5, a brief cold letter from Brereton appeared in the papers acknowledging the facts of the Irish situation. Sarah hoped the matter was ended. That evening Drury Lane was filled. As the curtain rose she made her entrance with John Philip. Instantly there was a violent burst of hissing and booing. She stepped to the footlights. The uproar increased, drowning the applause of her friends. Shouts struck at her from all over the house: *Off! Get off the stage! Off!* She stood rigid, too frightened to move, expecting any moment to be hit by a broken bottle, a lighted candle. When for a moment the jeering died down, she tried to speak. Shouts and catcalls rose in a storm tide. She was dimly aware of a man in the pit jumping up, his arms extended as if to support her, shouting, "For God's sake, Madam, do not degrade yourself by an apology, for there is nothing necessary to be said!" Then John Philip was beside her, propelling her offstage through waves of beating, receding sound; she felt her cheek strike his arm as she pitched forward, unconscious.

The curtain came down. Backstage everything was turmoil. Someone rushed for water, another for smelling salts.

As William worked to revive Sarah, John Philip angrily faced Brereton, insisting he go before the curtain and quiet the audience with an explanation. Glumly smiling, Brereton refused. John Philip and Mr. Aiken stared at him. Neither knew that Brereton was already far into serious mental illness, but they recognized something in him strange and frightening. Aiken turned and rushed onstage. The house quieted. The slanders against Mrs. Siddons were untrue, Aiken said in a rough, strong voice. She was generous and kind to anyone needing help.

Backstage, Sarah was on her feet again, taking deep gulps of air to steady herself — and refusing to go onstage again. Now or ever. John Philip pleaded; Sheridan pleaded, and at last William. Minutes later, her fear masked in a beautiful dignity, Sarah stepped onstage. The house went profoundly silent. She began to speak: "Ladies and gentlemen. . . . The stories which have been circulated about me are calumnies." Even her enemies were moved by her courage. The play began once more and continued uninterrupted.

Next morning the story made all the papers. Charges and countercharges were dragged up for rehashing. Then letters arrived from Mr. Digges and his son supporting Sarah. Mr. Woodfall of the *Chronicle* noted the charges against Sarah, the facts which refuted them — and judged her innocent. The matter, he said, might now be dropped. But those who enjoyed the gossip preferred to believe their former idol "cold" and "stingy." Those words, like the word "genius," would be repeated of Sarah through her lifetime and beyond.

Chapter Ten

The Challenge of Fear

"I HAVE BEEN VERY UNHAPPY; now 'tis over I will venture to tell you so." Quick though she had been to share her triumphs with old friends, Sarah was unable to share humiliation. Now, months after her disastrous opening night, she was writing to the Whalleys. What she had gone through she summed up and dismissed — at least on paper. That done, she wrote of the children. Sally, said her mother, was "an elegant creature, and Maria beautiful as a seraph. Harry grows very awkward, sensible and well-disposed." Eliza, the youngest, was developing "the sweetest tuneful little voice you ever heard."

To the Whalleys what Sarah's letters conveyed most poignantly was the outpouring of her love and need for love. "Good God!" they read, "what I would give to see you both, but for an hour! How many thousand thousand times do I wish myself with you, and long to unburden my heart to you . . . thank God, we are all well. I hope you are both so, and happy . . . and that you will love me. . . ." And again, "would to God I could laugh with, or cry with, or anything with you, but for half an hour!"

To another friend she wrote: "Oh, for a piece of Langford brown bread!" She longed for talk with Tate Wilkinson "over a pinch of your most excellent snuff." And she knew as she wrote that her longing for the friends and food, the snuff and ale of her Bath and country touring days was a desperate longing for safety. Yet she could not write of the secret fear she lived with now.

It was her London friends — Holcroft and Elizabeth Inchbald, the Devonshires and Sir Joshua, the Parliamentary leaders Pitt, Burke and Fox — who could help her. Themselves renowned, they were wise in the ways of fame and misfortune. It was they who saw her on the stage, "unnerved and uncertain," as she continued through performances which began with hissing and insult, playing cautiously, repeating herself. Gone was the freshness, the daring, the spontaneity they had come to expect from Sarah's acting. Her London friends were the ones who could lead her to talk, to admit that she "had lost all enthusiasm, and actually sickened at the very idea of continuing to be an actress." They could urge her to accept what she later wrote the Whalleys: "A strange capricious master is the public." They could assure her that fame so spectacular as hers was bound to inspire vicious envy and that the public had a way of striking down the idols it had raised.

Not just her professional but her private life was troubled. There was little peace in Gower Street. William, restless without work, grew sharp and critical. Even at the theatre, other actors were startled to hear him openly and harshly criticize Sarah for what he thought were errors in her acting. If she spoke of her panicky impulse to quit acting, William was furious.

Mary, the Siddonses' once-trusted maid, who had been dismissed for defrauding them of a large sum meant for the grocer and fishmonger, drunkenly elaborated on what she had overheard and told tales in every pub and tavern she frequented of how William was unfaithful and abused Mrs. Siddons. The stories went the round of London.

Samuel Jackson Pratt, a man whom the Siddonses had thought a friend in Bath, now joined the chorus of detractors. They had lent Pratt more than five hundred pounds, and when Sarah asked if he could repay a small amount of it he replied by sending her a copy of his latest play with the request she have it produced for him. She had returned it, saying she could do nothing herself, but advising him to take the play to Sheridan or the managers of Covent Garden. Pratt was incensed. He shrilled about London that Mrs. Siddons was a monster of ingratitude who had climbed to fame on his shoulders and was now kicking him down. A man of little talent as a playwright, Pratt was gifted in writing scurrilous tidbits of gossip. He now made certain London knew the story of Sarah's younger sister, Anne Kemble.

A wild and eerie eccentric, Anne was nine years younger than Sarah. Not mad enough to be confined to an asylum, she was a tragedy to herself and her family. She was an alcoholic, constantly having to be bailed out of debt, constantly attaching herself to various religious fakes and quacks. Recently she had taken up Dr. Graham's new religion at the Temple of Hymen.

One afternoon William answered the doorbell, then came running back upstairs to Sarah. "It's about Anne!" he blurted. "She gave a lecture at the Temple and then ran into Westminster Abbey and tried to kill herself."

"Oh dear God!"

Quietly the Siddonses did what they could for Anne, who resisted every effort to help her. When she later was shot and injured in a tavern brawl and newspaper paragraphs blamed Sarah's avarice for her sister's sad plight, Anne published a letter saying, "my relations have never shut their hearts against me, and are now alleviating my misfortunes by the *tenderest attentions.*" It was ignored in a storm of Pratt's malicious paragraphs, and London buzzed anew with talk of Mrs. Siddons' hard, uncaring stinginess. Imagine, said the eagerly jealous, the rich Mrs. Siddons letting her sister live in such degradation!

Elizabeth Inchbald could stammer in her sunny voice, "There, d-don't cry, dear heart, every family h-has a w-wild one," and Sarah was briefly comforted. She learned, as she later wrote the Whalleys, that her troubles were "the touch-stone to prove who were really my friends," but nothing helped dispel the wordless, haunting fear she was living with.

Nor could she lose the fear in her work, for it focused there. Night after night she drove herself onto the stage, fighting the impulse to run from the watching eyes that lined the house. She dreaded the moments when she was alone onstage. Then she felt stripped by a thousand probing eyes that judged not her acting, but Sarah Siddons, human being. She said her lines and repeated her gestures while reviewers began calling her "guarded and methodical." They noted a sense of effort in her work and found it cold and declamatory.

Sarah paced the gardens of Bedford Square. She walked through Covent Garden Market with its country scents of cabbage and flowers. She fled into the dusty serenity of St. Paul's and knelt, trying to think the problem through. What was the matter with her? In everything she did, everywhere she turned this year something went wrong. Why? She remembered the safe feeling of Bath; perhaps she should have stayed there. Yet she had known she must leave that safety to accept new challenges — even the challenge of fear itself. But it was the normal actors' fear she had meant, not this she now fought! She rose to go. But when did life give certain answers? She had asked for challenge. She knelt again and prayed.

Sheridan stared out the windows of his office and sipped his brandy. His veteran leading man, Gentleman Smith, was at him again. He had noticed, said Smith, that Mrs. Siddons appeared to be weary. Would it not, in view of the — ah — surely lowered box-office returns, be wise to consider that charming young actress he had mentioned before, Dorothy Jordan? As a second to the incomparable Mrs. Siddons, of course.

A few days later, in conference with Sarah, Sheridan broke off his discussion of plays to comment on the change in her. "Can't you ease up, be less fearful and cautious when you play?" He smiled teasingly. "Your public has forgiven you, you know."

"Forgiven me? For what? For their own damnable lies about me?"

"For their envy of your fame."

Sarah's temper flared. "Envy, malice, detraction! The fiends of hell! I have worked for my fame!"

Sheridan's eyes sparkled. So! The fire was still there. He debated a moment then took a gamble. "And I propose you work harder. I am casting you as Lady Macbeth. We'll open February second."

"No!" Suddenly pale, Sarah leaned against his desk. Her friends had been urging her to play one of Shakespeare's tragedies. Her enemies had been saying publicly that she "shrank from these great plays . . . from a sense of weakness, knowing that contact with this grand work would shiver her reputation like glass." She would be alone on-stage for her opening scene, alone in the famous sleepwalking scene except for two figures hidden in shadow at the side. "No, if I were to play Lady Macbeth — and fail — it would destroy me."

"You will not fail."

John Philip was elated when he heard the news. "Aha!" he thundered, "at last a play worth doing. We can now leave the claptrap to the Dolly Jordans."

"What do you mean by that?"

"You have not heard then? Hmph! All talking about it backstage." John assumed a pose typical of Gentleman Smith. "Ah, hmmm, what Drury needs is more comedy. Now there's that excellent and pretty little thing, Dolly Jordan." John laughed. "She is a pretty wench, too. And mark you, they will be engaging her for Drury before long."

Sarah winced. Was she slipping so badly? Then she dared not try Lady Macbeth. But if John were to play Macbeth he would help her. Her hopes for that were disappointed. Mr. Smith held first rank in the company and he chose to assert his right to the part. Sheridan assured Sarah of his confidence in her ability to overcome the disadvantage.

She began to work haunted by the fame of Mrs. Pritchard, who had played the role with Garrick. Never since her Bath days had Sarah followed tradition in a role; now she was tempted. She studied old reviews, pictures, sketches of the Garrick-Pritchard production. John Philip, glancing at an engraving of the famous pair in the dagger scene, hooted with laughter. "They look like the butler and the housemaid quarreling over the carving knife!"

"Mrs. Pritchard was celebrated in the role."

"Ha! I'm told the lady never burdened her mind with reading any words but her own, and never troubled herself with knowing what took place on the stage when she was off."

That settled it. Line by line Sarah began her study of the play, making careful notes as she searched for answers to the character: What were the forces that drove this woman to violence? What was the essence of her relationship to Macbeth? To the other characters? Sarah remembered her own horrified reaction to the character when she had studied her long ago in Cheltenham. Now she must open herself to that terror again no matter how it might shake her. The more she studied the less sure she became. Her concentration was shot through with dread of those scenes onstage alone.

Then Sir Joshua offered his help on costumes. Sarah admitted some — but not all — of her worry about the first scene. Lady Macbeth must enter alone, reading a letter. The character must have an immediate impact. Sarah talked of what she planned in the sleepwalking scene. There should be an eeriness about it, yet the movement must be real. In contrast to the way it had been played before, Sarah intended to play it according to her own observations of sleepwalkers. "They perform all the acts of waking persons," she said. Sir Joshua listened and went to work.

The Night came: February 2, 1785. Talk had raced through London. Could Mrs. Siddons equal Mrs. Pritchard or would she give one of her recently cold, methodical performances? The house was jammed. When Sarah finished her makeup, she asked her dresser to leave. A moment later in the hall, Sheridan stopped the dresser, his eyes sharply questioning. The girl shook her head worriedly. "She sent me out, sir, so's she could be alone. Very nervous she is tonight, sir."

Sheridan drew a delicate gold watch from his pocket. Almost curtain time. He moved a step or two away, then turned quickly and hammered on Sarah's dressing room door. "Mrs. Siddons, I must speak with you!"

"No!"

Sheridan knocked again. She must admit him, he insisted, it was a matter of the most serious nature. Sarah, fighting to make herself concentrate within the character, able to think only of that moment when alone she must enter and continue no matter what the reaction of the audience, at last flung open her door. "Please — go away!"

Sheridan pushed inside. "I am told by Mr. King that you intend to do the sleepwalking scene in a way that breaks all tradition." Sarah nodded. "I beg you, Sarah, do not introduce this new business. Go back to the way Mrs. Pritchard did it."

Furiously, Sarah refused. Sheridan argued, he beseeched. It would be presumptuous of her to change the traditional business of the scene. He begged her not to be obstinate.

Almost shaking with rage, Sarah pushed him out. The house had gone quiet. The curtain was up. She must concentrate, get into the mind of Lady Macbeth. There was no time. The play had started. She rushed to the prop table; in God's name where was the letter? Someone shoved it into her hand. She took her place in the wings, trying to hold down her fury. Damn Sheridan! In the flickering glow of the sidelights she read the first lines of the letter to herself. Out of long habit, her own emotion flowed into that of the character — damn all those who stood in the way of Macbeth! All hail Macbeth!

Her cue came.

Like a shock of evil she strode onstage. Her black gown was bordered from shoulder to hem in a streak of blood-red silk. Her face and body were vibrant with barely controlled emotion. Whatever their predisposition to hiss or applaud, the audience was struck into silence.

As the scene mounted to its climax Sarah's voice rang against the back walls in an ecstasy of evil. In his box Sheridan sat unmoving, tears of excitement in his eyes as the house around him exploded into shouting, stamping applause.

Speaking to no one, Sarah went into her dressing room and shut the door. As she changed for her final scene, the fear returned for a moment. Did she dare play it as she believed? Fear. She tried to put it down. No, stay open to it — Lady Macbeth is torn by fear and guilt. This is the depth of night in the murky reaches of the castle, in her own soul. She feels again the blood of the murdered King on her hands . . .

Sarah moved onto the stage. Again her entrance struck the audience with shock. Here was no traditional Lady Macbeth drooping about in languid sleepy movement, clinging always to the candle she held, speaking in enfeebled tones. Here was a woman moving as if awake, in terrible agitation. Yet there was an eeriness about her. The soft white nightdress moved like a shroud around her as she walked. She set the candle down. In agony she tried to wash the blood from her hands. A shudder went through the house. No actress had ever played the scene this way before — it was triumphantly right.

As if in a trance Sarah returned to her dressing room. Standing before her mirror she began to untie the cord of her white cloak, still repeating, "Here's the smell of blood still!" Her dresser laid her hand on Sarah's arm. "Dear me, ma'am, how very hysterical you are tonight; I protest and vow, ma'am, it was not blood, but rose-pink and water; for I saw the property man mix it up with my own eyes."

Startled, Sarah turned to her, then threw her arms around the girl in an exuberant hug. "And, oh, ma'am, do listen!" said the relieved dresser. "They're still cheering."

" 'Thanks be to God who giveth me the victory!' " breathed Sarah. She had forgotten to be afraid of her audience.

There was a quick rap on her door and Sheridan stood before her. He raised her hand to his lips and bowed over it. "My dear Mrs. Siddons! I congratulate you — on your obstinacy."

After this triumph, Sheridan cast Sarah in another Shakespearean role, as Desdemona in *Othello* with John Philip playing opposite her. Neither audiences nor critics could quite believe that the actress whom they saw now was the murderous Lady Macbeth. Then she had seemed six feet tall, a woman of maturity and power. As Desdemona they saw a girl almost childlike in her gentleness. One critic spoke for all when he wrote: "In this wonderful transition from Lady Macbeth to the bride of Othello, Mrs. Siddons has shown her genius to be a star of the first magnitude."

But for a few days it seemed this might be Sarah's last appearance for the season. She woke the morning after her opening feeling stiff and feverish, aching in every bone and joint. She must have caught cold, she said, from the wet sheets on Desdemona's bed. William was furious. Someone should have checked on it, the stage manager, the prop man, someone. Apparently no one had, and Sarah had lain there, damp and chilled. The next day she was worse. To move was excruciatingly painful. Gravely, the doctor told William that Sarah had contracted a rheumatic fever. She must remain in bed, perhaps for a long time; he would leave some opium to relieve her pain.

After a few days of rest Sarah was better. Within two weeks she was back onstage. "Poof!" she said to William's fuming, "I have health to sell." Even so, she was very tired. The strain of the season's difficulties, her battle against her own fears, and her illness had left their mark. She had subtly changed and her audience sensed it. When she played Rosalind in *As You Like It* there was a luminous quality about her that brought smiles but not laughter. One critic remarked that her comedy was only the smile of tragedy. Even James Boaden, who had seen her in every role with undiminished enthusiasm, noted that in Rosalind's escape to the Forest of Arden, "like a stricken deer, she comes into retirement to languish of a wound." He sensed that some quality was missing.

The melting tenderness which had so caught old Thomas Sheridan's heart was gone. In its place a new quality began to emerge from the fears and victories of this year — the power to reveal human truth in all its depths and high-lights.

In the spring Sarah knew she was again pregnant. Four children and a fifth on the way. And she knew she must depend on her favor with the public to care for them. Talking to Elizabeth Inchbald, she repeated what she had said to the Whalleys: "How wretched is the being who must depend on the stability of public favor."

"I d-don't," said Elizabeth. "I d-depend on s-stocks and b-bonds."

Sarah laughed. "And put a basket of gold coins on your hall table for anyone who wants to help himself."

"That's my d-dare to Fate," grinned Elizabeth.

But Elizabeth had neither children nor husband to support since Josephs Inchbald's death. The profits from her writing were her own. Sarah knew that not even William could manage financially without her. And she knew the answer. "I'm going on tour for Tate Wilkinson."

"R-rest is what you ought to do."

"I can earn as much in two months on tour as I can all winter in London." Sarah had determined her course. She would take on all the work she could get until she had put by ten thousand pounds for William to invest. After that, no matter what happened to her, the children would be secure. The resolve went deep; she would not be dependent on public favor one hour longer than necessary.

Audiences in the provincial theatres received her joyfully. And Sarah, released from the pressures of London, let herself swing with the tides of fortune or misfortune and laugh like the country trouper's child she once had been.

Playing Juliet one night in Manchester, she started the famous potion scene. In tense silence the audience followed her to the moment when Juliet drinks the mysterious drug which will send her into a living death. Sarah took the cup in her hands. Her voice rang with exultation: "Romeo, I come! This do I drink to thee!" Slowly she raised the cup to her lips. Suddenly a man in the galleries, unable to bear the suspense, shouted in his West Country accent, "Soop it oop, lass! Soop it oop!" For an instant there was silence, then as one, audience and Sarah collapsed into shouts of laughter.

All that summer, in spite of her pregnancy, she journeyed "over bogs and stones in a rattling coach" across the English countryside. Tate thought her the best of troupers. "She never heeds trouble," he said. Even if she were ill, if "possible to rise from her bed, she is certain in her duty to the public." If the wagon following with her costumes failed to arrive in time for the show, she simply asked Tate what play it was possible to do and did it, "never saying such a play will do better than another, or such a part would be too fatiguing." Tate, having dealt with a succession of temperamental touring stars, was able to appreciate Sarah's staunch dependability.

One morning she woke to find William holding a bunch of flowers in his hand. "Time you woke, Sally. It's your birthday."

Sarah sat up. "Why, so it is — my thirtieth. Sid! I am thirty years old!" Astonishing, she thought, to feel no different, and she scrambled out of bed to dress for the day's journey.

Sarah returned to London, her weariness deepening as her body grew heavier in pregnancy. She found Drury Lane agog with the news that Sheridan had engaged Dorothy Jordan. It was, said Sheridan, a hunch. London was in the mood for comedy. The guilt and despair so many Englishmen had felt over the war against the American colonies was wearing thin. Now people wanted to laugh.

Backstage, the talk was all of Jordan's fabled temper, of Jordan's formidable mother who could make life unbearable for rival actresses. The tale was told of how as one such rival performed at York, Mother had sat in the wings holding her apron over her eyes and saying loudly to anyone near that she could not bear to watch that *fright* onstage, *it* was so horrid.

Whatever the tales of Dorothy Jordan, the implication was clear that the anti–Siddons-Kemble group had found its heroine. Dubiously, Sarah attended Dorothy's opening night, October 18, 1785. Like the rest of that sparse house she knew before an act of *The Country Girl* was over that the small, curly-haired Mrs. Jordan was a true and rare comedienne. Watching her rollick across the stage, evoking a sure laughter from them all, Sarah knew that Drury Lane had a new great actress and that she at last had a rival worthy of the name.

Chapter Eleven

Revolution

DOROTHY JORDAN burst on the London scene in a roar of laughter that continued through the season. Sheridan was delighted. James Boaden wrote: "Certainly no lady of my time was ever so decidedly marked out for comic delight. She seemed as if formed to dry up the tears which tragedy had so long excited." And Sarah said to a friend, "We have a great comic actress now, called Mrs. Jordan; she has a vast deal of merit."

Whatever friendship or understanding might have grown between Drury Lane's two leading actresses, Gentleman Smith and his cohorts helped to stunt it. When Sheridan, anxious to profit from the trend to comedy, cast Sarah in a comic role, Mrs. Lovemore in *The Way to Keep Him*, Sarah responded happily if tactlessly that they would make comedy as fashionable as tragedy at Drury. Smith and his group immediately chose to regard the statement as an act of war and made Dorothy Jordan the innocent spearhead of their campaign against Sarah and John Philip.

Sarah was determined to make Mrs. Lovemore proof she could play comedy successfully. But she wished again, as she had many times, that John Henderson would play it with her. Their intuitive response to each other made a play into a sparkling game, the speed and bounce of lines back and forth as enjoyable to the audience as to the players. It was not to be. Helping her into the carriage after final rehearsal, William spoke quietly. "Sally, I wish you didn't have to know it now but there's no keeping it; John Henderson died today."

The next evening, November 26, as heavy in spirit as she was in body, Sarah played Mrs. Lovemore. She was not surprised that critics referred to her "assumed gaiety" and she was amused by one gentleman's defense of her acting. Ah well, said he, what if Mrs. Siddons could not play comedy so well as tragedy, who would wish to see "a fandango danced by the Empress of Russia"? No comments concerned Sarah deeply at this moment for there were more important things to think of. Her baby was almost due, and John Henderson's family must be helped. Immediately she wrote to Henderson's friends at Covent Garden that she would be honored to give a benefit for his family.

On the day after Christmas, 1785, Sarah's son George was born, "healthy and lovely as an angel," she said, and the house in Gower Street filled with gifts and notes of congratulation. The King and Queen wrote to say they wished to command a performance of *The Way to Keep Him* but they hoped Mrs. Siddons would not consider playing again until she was quite strong.

Two months later, on the night of February 26, 1786, carriages lined the streets near Covent Garden. It was the night of John Henderson's memorial benefit. The great of London theatre came together on one stage as Sarah played Belvidera and Frances Abington acted her famous role of Lady Racket. Sarah was comforted to know that James Boaden remembered how beautifully she and Henderson had played together and mourned with her for what could never be again.

In early June, Sarah set off on another tour for Tate Wilkinson. He had booked her only for his larger theatres. Immediately there was an uproar throughout the smaller towns. Audiences threatened to boycott all Tate's theatres unless he brought them Mrs. Siddons that very summer. Sarah good-naturedly agreed, and presently she was racketing over the countryside in a post chaise while Tate galloped after with the costumes and props.

It was in Leeds that Sarah gave perhaps her most startling performance of Lady Macbeth. The evening was hot and humid. Before the sleepwalking scene, which was her last in the play, she sent out for a pot of ale, assuming it would be left in her dressing room. But the tavern potboy, eager to serve the great actress, marched into the theatre, past the startled stage crew, and onto the stage.

Sarah had just put down the candle and begun the tragic business of washing the imagined blood from her hands. "Here's yer ale!" beamed the boy, thrusting the foaming tankard toward her outstretched hands. She tried to wave him off the stage, and turning away continued with the lines of the play: "Out, damned spot!" she moaned in a hoarse dramatic whisper. "Out, I say!"

"But I've brung yer ale!" the boy whispered back. Suddenly ale and tankard went flying as the boy was yanked offstage by one of the crew. Sarah joined the audience in helpless laughter.

In another town, the stage crew had assembled the scenery in a different position than usual. There was no time to rehearse with it. Sarah entered and played a deeply pathetic scene carrying her baby in her arms. Then, building to a tragic exit, her baby cradled tenderly in her arms, she turned with a dramatic sweep. The baby's head struck the doorpost with a resoundingly wooden crack. Splinters flew. For a second there was horrified silence, then howls of laughter echoed back and forth from pit to stage.

By August, Sarah was beginning to tire, and even Tate Wilkinson's enthusiasm for touring was nearly exhausted. "Good God!" he muttered, trailing after her, "what real fatigue!" When the tour was over, Sarah thankfully accepted Lord and Lady Harcourt's invitation to rest at their country house, Nuneham Manor.

In October, Sarah returned to a troubled theatre. With Sheridan increasingly busy in Parliament, Tom King had taken on more management responsibility. Bickering was rife. King blamed Sheridan for lack of money for repairs, costumes, scene paint.

"What the devil does Sheridan do with all the money?" William sputtered over his breakfast kippers and bacon.

"This, for one thing!" Sarah pointed to an article in the morning paper telling of Sheridan's opposition to the government's proposed tax on cotton. "It says Mr. Sheridan has traveled to Lancashire and seen for himself the dire poverty of the people there."

"And if he doesn't pay more attention to his theatre, his actors will be in dire poverty."

Sarah nodded. She knew how worried the Drury actors were. Unlike her, many of them refused or were unable to get country touring jobs. By the hardest kind of work she had now reached her goal of ten thousand pounds only to find rising prices had undercut the value of the money. Sheridan, to whom they all looked for help, was himself trapped between rising costs and falling box-office returns.

It was, said Sheridan, a strange time, a kind of limbo. Events in France were moving almost certainly to revolution. Theatre there reflected the turbulence. "Here in England," said Sheridan, "our government, our society both need reform — yet London wants laughter." Even laughter was having a rough time of it at Drury Lane, for Mrs. Jordan was proving as undependable as she was hilarious. And there seemed to be no good new plays.

"You should write one," suggested Sarah. "It's been too long since you have."

"I've no time." Sheridan's face was flushed and puffy.

He was drinking too much and driving himself too hard. His Parliamentary speeches revealed the arduous work he put into assembling the facts that underlay the brilliant words he used to attack corruption and demand reform. Yet he seemed unable to reform his own theatre.

John Philip Kemble, who had no mind for politics and rarely bothered to read a newspaper, nevertheless admired Sheridan greatly, and was one of his staunchest allies at Drury Lane. When infrequently his wrath was stirred — usually in a disagreement over theatre policy — John expressed it in his own lofty style. On one occasion when he and Sheridan were at a party, John Philip arose at the height of his anger and with stately precision hurled a wine decanter at Brinsley's head. Shortly after, they departed together in excellent spirits. In more serious moments, John was learning much about theatre from Sheridan, as well as from his own growing collection of original play manuscripts and books on dramatic theory and history.

Sarah, too, was continuing to study, and perhaps to learn as much in these dull seasons as in the more brilliant ones. She experimented with roles in new plays, and though the plays might be poor, she learned from the variety they afforded her. In her familiar roles, audiences found her always worth seeing again. Never taking her ability for granted, she spent the morning of each performance in careful, questioning study of the play. Each time, she said, she found new meanings, things she ought to have noticed before but had not, ideas that subtly colored her work.

As a result her playing remained fresh. When she acted

Belvidera, audiences were still "electrified" by the moment when her husband threatened to stab her and she defied him, flinging herself into his arms and crying, "Now then, kill me!" When she repeated Zara in *The Mourning Bride,* the character was even more "a magnificent tigress" than at first playing. After Sarah acted the role more than a hundred times, a member of the audience commented that the immediacy and painful physical reality of her acting made him feel deeply "for the agony and torture under which a fellow-creature suffered."

Her love for old friends remained fresh, and her longing to be with them. Fascinated by the first balloon flight in 1783, Sarah was impatient that flight had not quickly become practical and travel a simple matter of floating from town to town. In a moment of loneliness for the Whalleys, she wrote, "Surely the converse of good and gentle spirits is the nearest approach to heaven we can know," and added, "What a thing a balloon would be! but the deuce take them."

If Dorothy Jordan's appearances did not always take place as scheduled, they were at least frequent enough to give Sarah more evenings for friends and personal life. Hesitantly at first, then with growing assurance as she observed the very obvious delight of her guests, Sarah began giving small dinner parties and "evenings" at home in Gower Street. Soon the politicians Fox and Burke, Sir Joshua Reynolds, the Sheridans and others as famous joined the Siddonses' long-time friends to dine on thick grilled mutton chops or roasted sirloin of beef with asparagus, and salads made according to Sarah's favorite recipe, the greens and herbs carefully chosen so that "all should fall into their place like the notes of music." There might be a tureen of the Shakespeare Tavern's luscious turtle soup sent over for the occasion. Dessert might be hot buttered apple pie or a stack of the creamy thin pancakes sauced with wine and chopped orange peel called a Quire of Paper.

Sarah's butcher was as pleased as her guests with this newly evident social life. He confided to Tom Haydon, the painter, that there "never was such a woman for chops! . . . the Kemble family — the gentlemen, sir, — rump-steaks and kidneys in general was their taste; but Mrs. Siddons, sir, she liked chops."

The talk that went about the table was as rich as the food, of politics and theatre, art and poetry, and the people who made them. Sarah summoned her courage to return the calls of the many people whose carriages had lined the street before her home when first she became famous and who had proved their loyalty when she was the butt of public scorn. She was still too often the subject of jealous gossip to be comfortable among strangers and reacted to their stares with head-high dignity.

At times, shy and insecure without a role to play, Sarah was dismayed to hear herself answering a simple question in the rhythms of formal stage poetry. When the Edinburgh barristers held a ceremonial dinner in her honor, she was asked if the beef were too salty. She smiled and shook her head. Then with a panicky feeling that that was not answer enough, she intoned, "Beef cannot be too salt for

me, milord." On a similar occasion, when the waiter gave her
a glass of water, she said with unintentional stage cadences,
"You've brought me water, boy; I asked for beer." Her
critics were quick to make public jest of her words.

One group among whom Sarah was completely at ease
was the Sunday afternoon crowd at the Twisses'. Her sister
Frances had quit the stage to marry Francis Twiss, a drama
critic, and the two had set up a household where good food
and talk soon drew a circle of writers, artists, and theatre
people. Sunday afternoons at the Twisses' became a joyous
interlude for Sarah and John Philip, for Sheridan and Holcroft and Elizabeth Inchbald. And they drew others of
London's young creative radicals.

Over their beef and ale they argued and laughed and re-
made the world as they would have it, a world of love and
freedom, equality and brotherhood. "God himself has no
right to be a tyrant," said young anarchist William Godwin, confessing that he was now a member of the new
political club, the Revolutionists. Sheridan announced he
was a committee member of the Society of the Friends of
the People. Amelia Alderson, who would later marry John
Opie the painter, hotly insisted that men had no right to
be tyrants, either, and take over their wives' earnings or
force them to have a dozen children. Practical reform was
the thing, claimed Elizabeth Inchbald. For example, her
new play, *These Things Are,* was an ardent plea for prison
reform. And William Godwin observed that he and his
friend, Mary Wollstonecraft, not only agreed that women
should have equal rights but felt that marriage was out-

moded and degrading. Love was the only force to hold people together.

Here Sarah could indulge in the comedy she loved. "Make fast the doors!" she would shout and then launch into a lugubrious rendition of *The Ballad of Billy Taylor* or a speech in the character of Sir Anthony Absolute that left the company aching with laughter.

At times these afternoons left Sarah wishing half-guiltily that William were younger or that he had some creative or intellectual interest on which to hone his mind. He was growing more stodgy, more raspingly critical. He did not care to remake the world; he cared how much money Sarah earned in the world as it was. At his best, William was still the amiable, easy-hearted actor she had married. At other moments he seemed an almost-old man resentful of his wife's vitality and fame.

In 1787 the circle was enlarged by another old acquaintance. Friends in Bath had written that Thomas Lawrence was now coming to London to set up his studio. The Siddons and Twiss families immediately welcomed Lawrence into their homes. He had gained considerable note as a painter by this time; he was an extraordinarily handsome young man, "beautiful as an angel," some said, a fine athlete and dancer, reserved and courteous in manner. To William, the painter was just another pleasant young artist. To Sarah, he was Tom Lawrence who seemed always to bring her luck.

She respected his flashing skill and his disciplined work habits. And she resolved to help make his London debut successful. She spoke of him to friends, introduced him to wealthy and famous people who might commission sketches or paintings, and included him in parties she gave. With affectionate pride she watched his swift rise in London's art world.

Thomas Lawrence, not yet twenty but worldly beyond his years, looked at Sarah in a way she had never known. He saw her as William never could, with an artist's eye and a boy's adoration. He saw her as she was, at thirty-two one of London's most beautiful women, still slim and lithe as a girl, her dark eyes continually changing expression under the long curling lashes which so fascinated her children. Welcomed into the family, Lawrence saw a gentle, laughing, motherly woman hidden from outsiders. Repeatedly he sketched and painted her, in informal clothes and casual attitudes, and gave her an image of herself more alive and exciting than she had held before, when she had called herself Sarah Siddons, "matter-of-fact woman" and family wage earner.

During this year London's attention turned from painting and theatre to politics. The rhythm of London life began to quicken. On the eighth of February, 1787, Richard Brinsley Sheridan and Warren Hastings were names in all the papers. Sheridan, the day before, had risen in Parliament to charge Hastings, the former Governor-General of India, with corruption, oppression and torture of native people under British rule. When Sheridan concluded, "the whole House, the members, peers, and strangers, involuntarily joined in a tumult of applause." Parliament voted to impeach Warren Hastings. Sheridan was promptly involved in preparation for the impeachment trial and his theatre spun into deepening chaos.

It appeared, in fact, that revolution might come to Drury Lane before it came to France. Revolt centered around Mrs. Jordan. She was rebelling against Tom King, who in turn disapproved of her morals, costumes, and language. Mrs. Jordan hated Mrs. Siddons and the Kembles, and fought with Miss Farren and Mrs. Crouch, insisting they were given parts which should be hers. "Why don't you dismiss the woman?" demanded John Philip over a glass of wine with Sheridan.

"As you well know," sighed Sheridan, "Dolly Jordan is the mistress of Richard Ford, and as you may not know, Richard Ford's father holds a mortgage of thirty-one thousand, five hundred pounds on my theatre! Besides, she can play comedy as no one else can — when she chooses to play." The battle cooled briefly when Dorothy Jordan quit before the season's end and dashed to Edinburgh where she gave birth to Ford's child. Or, as the Edinburgh papers put in the shipping news column: "The Jordan from Edinburgh — a small sprightly vessel — went out of London harbor laden — dropt her cargo in Edinburgh."

Presently Sarah became involved in a gently tactful battle with Bertie Greatheed, now grown and true to his promise to write a play for her. He had presented her a tragedy, *The Regent*. She tried to suggest she was wrong for the part; another actress might be better. Bertie refused to consider it. Privately, Sarah said of the heroine Bertie had written: "This woman is one of those monsters (I think them) of perfection, who is an angel before her time, and is so entirely resigned to the will of heaven, that (to a very mortal like myself) she appears to be the most provoking piece of still life one ever had the misfortune to meet . . . and she is so pious that we are satisfied she looks upon her afflictions as so many convoys to heaven, and wish her there, or anywhere but in the tragedy."

Bertie revised his play until Sarah agreed to play the "milksop lady." *The Regent* opened on the evening of March 20, 1788. The next day Sarah was suddenly taken ill and suffered a miscarriage. With another actress in the part, Bertie's tragedy struggled five more nights before collapsing.

In April real tragedy struck. Six-year-old Eliza, the blue-eyed daughter whom Sarah had called "the most entertaining creature in the world," became ill, and on April 16 she died. Eliza was buried in the blue and white Marylebone Church and Sarah went home to the quiet house in Gower Street. For the second time, Sarah had experienced the death of a child. But Frances Amelia had died as a baby; Sarah had had six years of knowing and loving Eliza. In her grief there seemed only one place she wanted to be — Guy's Cliffe — and when the season ended, Sarah sought the rest and peace she always found there.

When fall came she returned to the Drury Lane turmoil. Sheridan spent all his working hours preparing for the Hastings trial. He had no time for the squabbles of his actors, no time for anything but dropping by the box office to pick up what cash he needed. The trial was scheduled to open February 13, 1788.

With Sheridan's wife, Elizabeth, Sarah took her place in the galleries of scarlet-draped Westminster Hall. The solemn pageantry began. The procession entered, headed by Mr. Burke walking alone, a parchment scroll in his hand. Mr. Fox and Brinsley Sheridan followed. A spectator commented, "There Siddons . . . looked with emotion on a scene surpassing all the imitations of the stage" as Burke pronounced the charge: "I impeach Warren Hastings of high crimes and misdemeanors . . . I impeach him in the name of all the Commons in Great Britain whose national character he has dishonored. . . . I impeach him in the name of the people in India, whose laws, rights, and liberties he has subverted, whose properties he has destroyed, whose country he has laid waste and desolate. . . . I impeach him in the name of human nature itself."

Sarah gripped Elizabeth Sheridan's arm while tears rose to her eyes. What drama could be greater than this — the Commons of England challenging their own government's right to misuse its imperial power over the people of another land? No wonder Elizabeth Sheridan spoke so rapturously of her husband's "genius, eloquence, and *goodness.*"

For months the trial went on, while the backstage war at Drury reached a crest and broke with the resignation of Tom King's strongest backer, Gentleman Smith. King resigned and left London the same day. Drury Lane swung back and forth without an anchor. Then Ford sold his interest, Sheridan gained full control, promptly appointed

John Philip as his manager, and returned to work on his forthcoming speech at Warren Hastings' trial.

The trial was reaching its climactic moments. Sheridan's speech for the prosecution was set for June 3. All of London, it seemed, wanted to be present for this confrontation between Hastings and the man who accused him. By midnight of June 2, the coffeehouses and taverns near Westminster Hall were crowded with sleeping people. By six-thirty the next morning the Palace Yard was jammed with people waiting for the doors to open. In the struggle to get places several ladies lost caps and shoes and entered barefoot rather than miss the proceedings.

Sheridan's speech, however, was not aimed at this eager audience. He spoke directly and with the utmost gravity to the Lord Chancellor, the judges and peers — astute men, most of them, and trained in the law. At the conclusion of Sheridan's speech several days later, Edward Gibbon, the historian and a fellow member of Parliament, referred to it as "that display of genius which blazed four successive days."

For more than eighteen months Sheridan had poured out his energy on the trial. He could have profited handsomely from the sale of his speech to a publisher. Predictably, he refused. He held to his belief that a profit on the side from his Parliamentary position would destroy his integrity. That his integrity might be equally compromised by his irresponsibility toward his creditors or his actors was an argument that failed to move him. He fully intended to pay them — eventually.

Luckily, in John Philip Kemble, Sheridan had a manager

who was strong enough to bring a restless peace and growing profit to Drury Lane. Plays were now mounted with studious care instead of the "scandalous squalor" King had permitted. Sarah greeted John's new power with mixed reactions. That John would manage Drury well and honestly she had no doubt. But she had qualms about his production policies. John was such a careful, studious actor and director; he pounced so joyously on the possibilities for intellectually accurate scenery and costuming. Would he forget the spirit of the plays he produced?

Sarah was cast in what became one of her most noted roles, Queen Katherine in *Henry the Eighth,* the part Samuel Johnson had hoped to see her play. John Philip's production was fraught with accuracy. No one could argue a single detail. Sarah could argue the acting with him. She must, she said, get inside the character, feel the character's emotions as her own.

"Nonsense," said John. "It makes the tears course down your nose."

"I was never more applauded than in Belvidera and I felt every word as if I were the real person!"

"It is not necessary to feel anything," said John with a superior smile, "only to study the character and to present the gestures and voice one has planned."

"Hah! That's what makes James Boaden say you walk your character around the stage as if you were teaching the audience how it should move and pronounce its words!"

"I am a classicist."

"And even in your most impetuous outbursts, you always

are so careful not to get your hair mussed or your clothes disarrayed. I lose all thought of such things in the whirlwind of passion!"

"You should not, you know." And John stalked from the room.

Sarah relied on study, too, but she knew the value of emotion in drawing actor and audience together in a communion of experience. When as Queen Katherine, she rose to denounce the Cardinal, her body and voice shot through with the fire of her anger, the applause was said to have literally shaken the walls. A young actor who had never met with her intensity onstage, came off shaky and sweating. "That woman plays as if the thing were in earnest," he whispered to another actor. "I would not for the world meet her on the stage again!"

Playing Volumnia with John Philip in the title role of *Coriolanus*, Sarah stole the show from him. It was a concept so brilliant in its originality that not only audience but other actors were caught in admiration. Charles Young, an actor, described the scene where Sarah entered to a background of military music. Instead of walking in cadence with the beat as customary, she "almost reeled across the stage; her very soul, as it were, dilating and rioting in its exultation, until her action lost all grace, and, yet became so true to nature, so picturesque, and so descriptive, that, pit and gallery sprang to their feet, electrified by the transcendent execution of the conception." It was again an instance of the fusion of mind, body and emotional fire that caused one observer to say, "her very body seemed to think."

Late that spring London celebrated King George's recovery from a siege of porphyria, a rare and serious illness which had caused him to be thought insane. Drury Lane and the other theatres joined in the festivities. Sarah read an ode on the occasion, written by a "furious zealot for liberty," which seemed to at least one prominent critic a celebration of what he regarded as unfortunate radical tendencies more than of George's return to sanity. Sheridan, listening as Sarah's voice spoke the words, "Long may he rule a willing land," grinned broadly as her voice rang out to the top galleries on the warning note of the last line, "But, oh! forever may that land be free!" She was unexpected sometimes, this supposedly cold and dignified genius!

Always now on opening nights — and often on others — Sarah knew the "seraphic eyes" of Tom Lawrence watched her every move. She knew he would come back after, joining those who visited in her dressing room, that he would speak in easy, appreciative phrases, assuaging the sting of William's criticism. Sitting before her mirror one night, she caught the reflected radiance of her face as she turned to greet him. Later, toweling off makeup, she felt her hands unsteady against her face.

She was very tired, she knew. Tired from the unceasing drive of work, from grief for Eliza, from the subtly abrasive tension within the theatre and with John Philip. The aching soreness of joints and muscles which had occasionally plagued her since the bout of rheumatic fever was recurring more often. She wanted to get out of London, to rest in the country. And she must, somehow, restore the closeness with William that seemed gone. Perhaps they should take a holiday, travel somewhere together.

With summer came news that changed England's mood and Sarah's with it. On July 14, 1789, the people of Paris stormed the Bastille prison. The revolution had begun. Radicals and liberals everywhere hailed it as "the greatest event . . . that has ever happened in the world." In August came the French Declaration of the Rights of Man. In London, Sheridan read the news with warm sympathy and excitement. These ideals, he thought, would surely bring freedom to all of Europe and reform to his beloved England. The young poet Wordsworth spoke for all artists and intellectuals of the day:

> *Bliss was it in that dawn to be alive,*
> *But to be young was very heaven!*

Sarah thought of her daughters, Sally and Maria, now in school in Calais on the French coast, and made a decision.

One afternoon in late summer she tried to explain it to Sheridan. They were two tired people who knew each other well. Little needed to be said. If Sarah, in her way, wanted to declare her freedom and leave Drury Lane, he understood. Eyes weary and bloodshot from the wine he used to escape his own tensions, Sheridan faced her. "We can play comedy," he said. "We're strong enough in that line to do without you." But John Philip stood before Sarah, making the odd humming sound that was his prelude to explosion and in wordless fury stalked from the room.

William agreed to a holiday in France, and Sarah began

planning the visit to Maria and Sally. Perhaps they might all enjoy some French theatre, visit Holland, talk together of France in the newness of its freedom. But first, William felt, Sarah must tour and earn more money. Through the winter she played provincial towns until by spring she was exhausted and ill. Her doctors approved the holiday, however, and in early summer the Siddonses sailed for Calais. Sarah found her daughters "improved in their persons, and (I am told) in their French." The four of them attended the theatre in Lisle where Sarah said, "though I know nothing of the language, the acting was so really good that it gave me great pleasure."

Back in Calais on July 14, one year from the beginning of the revolution and nine days after Sarah's thirty-fifth birthday, she watched the ceremony of the Civic Oath of the new constitution administered. "It was a fine thing. . . . I was extremely delighted . . . the idea of so many millions throughout that great nation, with one consent, at one moment . . . breaking their bonds asunder, filled one with sympathetic exultation, good will and tenderness. I rejoiced with them from my heart."

Chapter Twelve

New Winds from France

NEITHER THE SUNNY CLIMATE nor the revolutionary fervor of France improved Sarah's health for long. The deep fatigue and muscle pain continued. William grew annoyed; he wanted to be in London; he had business affairs to attend to. Sarah guessed there might be another reason but said nothing. Returning to England, William suggested they rent a cottage at Sandgate. From there he could travel to London while Sarah took the mineral baths and consulted her physician, Sir Lucas Pepys.

From Sandgate, in August, Sarah wrote Lady Harcourt that Sir Lucas "says my disease is entirely nervous. I believe I am much better, but I get on so slowly that I cannot speak as yet with much certainty. . . . Mr. Siddons leaves me here for a fortnight while he goes to town on business . . . I live in terror of being left alone so long." The former Hester Thrale, who had once thought Sarah a "leaden Goddess," was now married to an Italian musician named Piozzi. After hearing the rumors of William's unfaithfulness, Mrs. Piozzi commented, "Poor pretty Siddons! A warm heart and a cold husband are sad things to contend with, but she'll get through."

By autumn Sheridan and John Philip were urging Sarah to return to London. She hesitated. In spite of Sir Lucas' ill-tasting remedies she felt little better. But William had found a new house for them in Great Marlborough Street, "not so pretty as Gower Street," he had written Mr. Whalley, "but more among our friends" and "with plenty of closets, which the ladies in general seem fond of." He had seen to calling in painters and paperhangers, but there were bills to be paid. Sarah had not worked in more than a year.

Returning to London that December of 1790, Sarah entered a period when time lost all ordinary meaning. Too much was happening all at once. It would be true for many people through these coming years. Under their personal lives, time became a ragged music, its rhythm the swing of revolution and reaction.

For Sarah, the period began normally enough. London welcomed her back with full and cheering houses. At her opening performance, the audience sprang to its feet in a burst of applause which continued five minutes. Only later, at parties, were there murmurs of concern: *But how Mrs. Siddons has changed! So very much thinner, don't you think? Ah, yes, a languor in her face that speaks of illness.*

She was able to play only a few roles that season, but in April, William was writing Mr. Whalley that Sarah's benefit night had been "a golden letterday," bringing in £402, which was £60 over the record at Drury Lane. He glowed with ideas for spending it — travel in Switzerland and Italy, if only they could afford their own post horses.

Then Sheridan called his company together to hear an announcement. The Theatre Royal in Drury Lane had been condemned. It was old and unsafe, the authorities had ruled; it wanted too much repair. At the close of the season, on June 4, the theatre would be torn down. He was trying even now to raise money to build a new Drury Lane. Meanwhile, in October, the Drury company would move to the King's Theatre in the Haymarket, better known as the Opera House.

John Philip was elated. Sheridan's new theatre was already in the planning, he told Sarah. It would be bigger, better in every way. There would be machines to raise the scenery from below the stage or make it descend, machines for making storms and waterfalls.

"And for actors?"

John ignored her. "We shall have the great William Capon as designer. I envision scenery meticulous in its accuracy, expressing that for which Kemble was born — truth! There will be Gothic castles of turreted magnificence —"

"John! Truth is people. Truth is human. It has nothing to do with castles and waterfalls. Actors can create in a barn, an innyard, in the streets if they must!"

Humming like an angry bee, John strode from the room. On the night of her last performance Sarah wandered about the old theatre. The gilt was peeling, the stairways creaked, but it had held so much of splendor and greatness. She felt the worn uneven stage boards beneath her feet, as if for the first, rather than the last time, and noted the one Sheridan had already marked for the wreckers to save. It would be, he said, the first board nailed down on the stage of new Drury. Sarah was thankful her work was ending early. She would not have to be present that last night when Mr. Palmer would step before the curtain, his hand lifted for silence, and instead of "raising the dead" — the actors' term for announcing the next show — he would announce the death of Drury Lane.

Death was indeed the word Londoners were using. Here in this old theatre, they and their parents and great-grandparents had watched the best of England's actors over a hundred-year span. Here London had laughed at Kitty Clive, been captivated by the youthful love of Woffington and Garrick, wept with Sarah Siddons. They felt it quite appropriate that the papers should carry an obituary notice:

THE DEATH OF OLD DRURY

On Saturday night, of a gradual decay, and in the 117th year of her age, died old Madam Drury, who existed through six reigns, and saw many generations pass before her . . .

And in Great Marlborough Street, William wrote on of parties and plans. Sarah "last night did the honors of her house until two in the morning." Next day they were to dine with the Chevalier St. Michael, brother to the King of Poland who wanted Sarah to visit Warsaw.

But, thin and tired, Sarah went to Guy's Cliffe. It had become for her the childhood home where she was always welcome, where she could rest. Later she joined William at Nuneham Rectory, the house they had rented near the Harcourts, and picked up her modeling tools.

More than any pills or treatments, Sarah was finding solace for her nerves in working with clay. Encouraged by her friend Mrs. Damer, a well-known sculptor, Sarah tried it haphazardly at first, then with quickening interest. Pounding and pummeling, shaping and molding the clay with her hands she could give vent to much she felt and forget what she would otherwise be thinking.

It was difficult to forget the news for long. Without grain from France, the price of bread was rising. Many blamed the revolution and turned their anger on those who supported it. In late July, papers headlined the attack on Joseph Priestley, radical minister and scientist, friend of Holcroft and William Godwin. A mob had ransacked Priestley's chapel and his home, burned his books and manuscripts, destroyed his scientific instruments. Priestley had disappeared. Sarah shuddered. Was Holcroft in danger? Godwin? Sheridan?

When Sheridan and John Philip arrived for a visit in September, they found Sarah recovering from another miscarriage but willing to consider a schedule of work for the coming season. She would play no new roles, they decided, but repeat popular plays in her repertory.

Sarah asked about Priestley; had he escaped, was he safe? "Hidden," said Sheridan, "by his friends in the Lunar So-

Interior of the Drury Lane Theatre Royal as it appeared in 1792 before it was demolished.
(From the Raymond Mander and Joe Mitchenson Theatre Collection)

ciety, those now-suspect gentlemen who believe that learning is not to be had at our established universities but in the conversation of intelligent and questing men." Sheridan grinned. "Very dangerous. They meet each month near the full of the moon. James Watt and Josiah Wedgwood are members."

"Josiah Wedgwood?" Sarah had collected some of Wedgwood's pottery to study the clean, graceful lines of the figures modeled on his vases and urns.

John Philip yawned. "I don't know what you're talking of; I never read newspapers."

"But their headlines determine your life!" Sheridan began.

"I read Shakespeare and the classics," said John. "The devil with your Societies for this and that, the Friends of the Revolution. Yes, and Tom Paine and his *Rights of Man!*"

Before Sheridan could argue, Sarah excused herself. She had felt unwell since her miscarriage and had more sympathy at the moment with Mary Wollstonecraft's ideas on the rights of women.

In London, Sarah and the Drury company discovered the problems of the Opera House. It was enormous; the stage, built for operatic spectacle, dwarfed anything less. The actors had to slow their speech and shout to be heard. They had to exaggerate gestures to make them seen across the vast space. And what about entrances and exits? Should they, as opera singers did, walk onto the stage and up to the edge of the set, then assume their characters and begin the scene?

Or finishing a scene, deliver their final lines, then walk off backs to the audience and arms lifted "in the figure of a candlestick with two branches," as Boaden described it? Surely all truth of character must be lost.

Stubbornly refusing to believe there was no better answer, Sarah began experimenting. Already noted for the superb clarity of her pantomime, she now brought her knowledge of sculpture to the problem. She thought of the clean, flowing lines of the Greek figures on Wedgwood's pottery. Soon her audiences noted a change in her acting style.

Completely in character she would enter, "bowed with affliction" or perhaps "in a hurry of distraction," and then stop, as if caught for a moment in an attitude that spoke "wonders to the eye until a second rush forward brought her to the proper ground on which her utterance could be trusted." She eliminated hats, feathers, fussy details of costume, anything which might obscure the clear line of her movement. In simplicity she found the way to keep her acting human and true even in this vault of a theatre.

The season was scarcely settled into routine when Londoners were startled to read a notice in the papers: the French revolutionary government had decided on war with Austria and Prussia if the rulers of these countries made efforts to suppress the revolution. "A hundred thousand Frenchmen, brave and well armed" were "longing for the signal to attack." And, said the notice, "the people of England will offer up prayers for the success they know will one day be their own."

The people of England offered up prayers and curses. They

wanted no more war. The thought of French armies longing for attack filled them with dismay. King George's ministers shrieked their alarm. This was open invitation to revolution! And in England! This was what came of these political societies corresponding with revolutionists in France! Sarah watched the tension increase under Sheridan's smile. But little more than a month later, on January 30, a day when each year England commemorated with fasting and humiliation the beheading of King Charles I in the English revolution of 1649, Sheridan's theatre played, not tragedy, but two wild comedies.

The alarms sounded again. Such behavior, cried the conservatives, was calculated to "continue the miserable dupes of Paris" in their opinion that the English people would one day join them in revolution. Sheridan continued to press for reform in government. Bulletins and correspondence continued to fly back and forth across the Channel between writers, intellectuals, political societies. Then April arrived with the promise of summer's rest.

Sarah had nearly finished her season. Her brother, Stephen, now manager of the Edinburgh Theatre Royal, began pleading with her to act for him this summer. William groused about his rheumatism and investments. The newspapers headlined war. France had declared war on Austria to defend and spread the revolutionary crusade. Prussia joined Austria; Catherine the Great offered Russian troops. The armies of Europe were on the move. And in Paris and the countryside mobs rioted in the streets protesting the price and scarcity of food. With news of the riots Sarah forgot everything else. Dear God, she prayed, let us get the girls home safe.

When they arrived — Sally a sweetly dignified seventeen, Maria a grubby-handed thirteen — Sarah barely had time to greet them and see them off for summer in the country with Mrs. Piozzi before she had to leave for Scotland. Stephen had already scheduled her to act. As always, Scottish audiences flocked to applaud her, and Edinburgh seemed blissfully far from war and riot.

But the news reached even there. The citizen armies marched across France singing the words of the poet, Rouget de Lisle, "the day of glory is here. . . . To arms, citizens!" And suddenly they turned back from victory at the front; they marched on Paris. Frenzied mobs surged through the streets searching out presumed enemies of the revolution. Summary trials and executions killed more than a thousand people in a few days.

Sarah and many another English man and woman were appalled. Was this the dawning freedom they had hailed? They thought again of Edmund Burke's sarcastic comment on the French revolutionary leaders: "Amidst assassination, massacre, and confiscation . . . they are forming plans for the good order of future society." Thank God, she thought, remembering her own experiences with mob emotion, thank God the girls are safe!

Safe? There were letters from Mrs. Piozzi: Sally was having violent asthma attacks, coughing blood. The common specter of the time rose in Sarah's mind. So many young people died of lung disease — consumption, the doctors called it. Was Sally to be another victim? Sarah hurried home and gathered her family together in the house on Great Marlborough Street.

She liked this house William had found. It was old-fashioned, warmer and larger than the Gower Street place, with rooms enough for all the children, for parties and the rough games of boys. Listening to seven-year-old George one afternoon, Sarah had paused in the letter she was writing to note her perpetual astonishment at how much noisier boys were than girls.

Sally was soon better, and Sarah, too. Determined to regain her strength for a family that increasingly needed her efforts, Sarah had consulted another doctor. Her trouble, he found, was not all "nerves" but had a physical cause which could be treated. Soon Sally was writing to a friend, "my beloved mother is at length cured of her complaint, and quite an altered woman."

By the end of 1792 the new Drury Lane was rapidly taking shape, but Sheridan was more than ever elusive. He had no time for actors, builders or painters. Sarah knew he was busy and distracted; neither she nor the other irate Drury actors knew Sheridan was meeting secretly with the French emissary, Chauvelin, in desperate efforts to avert war between France and England. Less than a month later, on January 21, 1793, the imprisoned King of France was beheaded on the guillotine. Feeling in England ran strong against the revolution. All theatres closed for a night as a sign of mourning. In February, France declared war on England and Holland. An angry fright gripped England. It suddenly became "safer to be a felon than a reformer." Yet Sheridan continued in Parliament, quietly and with facts and accounts to back his words, speaking in behalf of justice and reform. He had no time to oversee the mounting bills, the construction delays at his theatre. The new Drury was not ready to open in the fall. The Opera reclaimed its house and Sheridan's actors took jobs where they could find them.

In her upstairs sitting room, while Thomas Lawrence sketched her, with the sound of the girls' chatter from below, Sarah debated what to do. She must work and that meant touring. But the provinces or Ireland? She wanted neither.

Lawrence put down his pencil. His work, coming to full maturity of skill and power, had earned him great fame. Far more sensitive and understanding toward women than most men of his day, Lawrence was noted for his revealing portraits of famous women. He drew from them a response that let him see and paint the human being under the façade of fashion.

Sarah looked at the drawing he held out. How surely he had caught her mood! "I must go to Ireland this winter," she said. Silent, Lawrence let her talk, of her need to work, of William's preference for the Irish tour on which he would accompany her. Both knew she would go; both knew they would miss each other deeply. Fourteen years apart in age, they were hardly aware of it. Lawrence was old for his years, Sarah young for hers. Both creative, emotional, music-loving, age was no barrier to their companionship. But they

were very different. Where Lawrence was capricious, un-
stable, continually rumored in love with one beautiful
women after another though he offered neither marriage
nor a serious relationship to any, Sarah was disciplined,
constant, devoted to her family. They found in these shared
domestic moments, Sarah often knitting or sewing, Lawrence sketching, an undemanding peace — and under the
peace an excitement neither could admit.

Sarah returned from her Irish tour, said Mrs. Piozzi,
"handsome, celebrated, enriched, adored." She was also "big
with child." But there would be time for her to play Lady
Macbeth at the opening of new Drury in April. She watched
in pleasant lethargy as John Philip dashed about supervising
details of this all-new production of *Macbeth*. She listened
in amusement to the bleats of protest that rose from the
actors playing the Witches when John announced they
would no longer be able to attract attention by fancy costumes. "But I have always worn a red stomacher and a
laced apron!" cried one. "I, too," wailed another, "and ruff
and mittens and a plaited cap!"

"You will now be distinguished only by the fellness of
your purpose," said John with resonant precision. "You will
have to *act!*"

Opening night, April 21, 1794, was a brilliant spectacle.
Londoners were eager to see the three Kembles, Sarah, John
and their youngest brother Charles, in this fabulous production in this marvelous new fireproof theatre. The audience
watched fascinated as an enormous iron fire curtain lum-

bered down. An actor hammered on it to prove its solidity. The curtain clanked up again to reveal a lake of real water and a cascading waterfall. The play finally began.

Actors and audience soon knew the days of Garrick's great acting style were over. Drury Lane was too big; it had all the problems of the Opera House. Publicly joining her brother's enthusiasm for the new theatre, Sarah privately welcomed a young actor by saying, "I am glad to see you at Drury Lane, but you are come to a wilderness of a place, and God knows, if I had not made my reputation in a small theatre, I never should have done it."

In Paris the guillotine thudded against the block forty to fifty times a day. Poor and young died as well as rich and aristocratic; no one was safe. The cannons of France blasted her neighboring countries. English reaction rose toward panic. And in Sheridan's theatre John Philip Kemble and Dorothy Jordan fought over the importance of their names on the playbill, and wondered why few people cared.

For Sarah it was a time of waiting. This baby was late and she knew it and worried. Then, three weeks after her thirty-ninth birthday, Sarah's baby was born and christened Cecilia. "A dear fat lump," Sarah wrote of her, "as perfect and healthful a baby as ever the sun shone on." And William crowed to a friend, "as fine a girl as if her father was not more than one-and-twenty."

William and the rest of the family went off to Margate for a holiday, insisting Sarah join them in September. She confided to a friend, "I wish they would go and enjoy themselves there and leave me the comfort and pleasure of

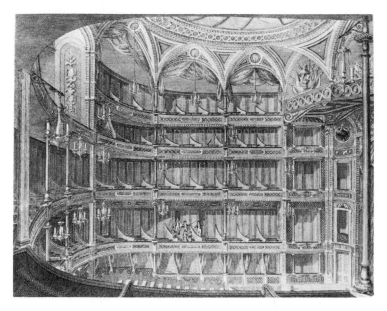

Interior of the new Drury Lane as it appeared on opening night, 1794. (From the Raymond Mander and Joe Mitchenson Theatre Collection)

remaining in my own convenient house, and taking care of my baby." She was especially fond of this fat, jolly child. Born into war and revolution, Cecilia called forth a special protectiveness from her mother. Lawrence, too, delighted in her, sketching her before she was even weaned.

There was a new note in Sarah's letters now. She was beginning to want something she had never had — a part of life that was her own. She knew she was influenced by all the talk from Mary Wollstonecraft and Amelia Alderson, but it was true, nonetheless. She wrote to a friend: "I have had no will of my own since I remember," and, "I shall never begin to live for myself I believe and perhaps I should not like it, were it in my power."

To Margate she went, however, and then to Edinburgh in answer to Stephen's pleas. Before she left, the house resounded with angry, worried voices. And Sheridan's name was in every other sentence. Writers, booksellers, members of political societies were being jailed for suspected revolutionary activity. Sheridan was standing firm, defending those unjustly accused, though he sickened, as most English liberals did, at the betrayal of early revolutionary ideals by the bloody Paris terror. Did Sarah know Tom Holcroft had been accused of high treason? That Sheridan would defend him? "If these men are convicted," shouted Amelia Alderson, "I shall emigrate to the free and unrepressive air of Philadelphia!"

With all the wit at his command Sheridan lashed at the foolishness of the evidence against Holcroft and the others. The juries refused to convict. But while he was helping to save the lives of Holcroft, Horne Tooke and others, Sheridan's own theatre life was floundering. Increasingly he sought relief in wine and love affairs. It was said about London he could not be trusted alone with any woman for five minutes. Sarah once teased him about it when he jumped into her carriage as she left the theatre. "Mr. Sheridan," she said with dry dignity, "I trust you will behave with all propriety. If you do not I shall have to call the footman to show you out of the carriage." Sheridan laughed briefly. They rode to her house almost in silence as if he had forgotten what he meant to say. Then Sheridan jumped down and bolted off. "Provoking wretch," Sarah murmured indulgently.

William, grumpy with gout and irritable at Sheridan's slow payment of Sarah's money, felt no indulgence at all — toward anyone. He was as annoyed as Sarah was delighted to have their house full of the noisy young — from small Cecilia to the group around Sally and Maria — banging in and out of the house, meeting to go on picnics, to go dancing. More and more often William sought the waters of Bath.

In spring of 1796 Sarah found her world in turmoil. The war was going badly. French troops thrust ever closer to England across the Low Countries of France and Holland. News of the Drury Lane squabbles were comic relief in the papers beside the columns of Napoleon's advances and Englishmen dead. Sarah became more tense and disturbed. When she was ill for a time, paragraphers gossiped she had gone mad. She was both amused and upset by the gossip. She wrote to Mrs. Piozzi: "I am studying *Vortigern* and *Almeyda;* and only scrawl these few lines for fear you have been frightened at some story of my biting or barking." But to another, she said: "I should laugh if it were not for the sake of my children to whom it may not be very advantageous to be supposed to inherit so dreadful a malady."

John Philip lived in constant, gloomy fury. Tradesmen refused colors for the scene painters, actors refused to play unless he guaranteed their pay. Sheridan owed Sarah large sums on back salary and could only promise to pay. She took to the provinces where the managers paid in cash. Then John Philip was arrested for one of Sheridan's theatre bills. Quickly released, he resigned as manager. William was threatening to see his lawyers. Yet when the fall season opened both Sarah and John continued with Sheridan. Wrote Sarah in midwinter: "Very few of the actors are paid, and all are vowing to withdraw themselves; yet still we go on." Miss Farren quit, Mrs. Jordan stayed home with the Duke of Clarence and their numerous children, the Popes refused to play. When Sarah finally stayed home the evening of a performance Sheridan rushed to her house in a carriage. One look at his harassed face and Sarah put down her sewing and went back to Drury Lane.

"Yet still we go on." Sarah's words summed up the essence of these years from 1790 to 1796. As they drew to a close nothing seemed settled, nothing begun, nothing ended. Yet beginnings and endings were taking shape.

These years had brought William from active manhood to the rheumatic edge of old age. They had brought Sally

*Mrs. Siddons as Mrs. Haller. Engraving after the
portrait by Sir Thomas Lawrence.
(From the Raymond Mander
and Joe Mitchenson Theatre Collection)*

and Maria home from France and to the first years of adult-
hood. The winds from France had blown cold over Sheridan's hopes; his political career was on the wane, his theatre
a shambles.

Thomas Lawrence was painting another portrait of Sarah.
Of Sarah as he knew her at home, warm, gentle, funny. He
thought of her singing a comic song for George, mending
a dress, cuddling small Cecilia. He painted her as he saw
her, young and alive with loving. And he posed her facing
directly toward him.

Chapter Thirteen

Thomas Lawrence

LAWRENCE'S FRIENDS had begun to worry about him. He brushed their questions aside. William Godwin wrote him: "I have felt considerable anxiety about you . . . now you hint to me that your uneasiness is sacred, and that no one must intrude upon it." There was really nothing Lawrence wanted to say, except to Sarah. He had tried to say it with paints and brushes. But her reaction when he had shown her the nearly finished portrait was unexpected.

It was a small picture, barely two feet square. She had looked at the face in the painting for a long time, then half-smiling, put it down. "It looks so young, so much too young." And her voice was as if she had said to a departing friend — I shall miss you. Lawrence was furious. She was younger than years could count, he insisted, at the very peak of her beauty. If that were so, Sarah had responded, then her beauty must soon go.

Someone called her from below stairs. They were getting ready for an after-theatre party. The cook wanted a word, the carpenters were putting up extra tables, she was needed. And Mrs. Siddons, experienced housewife and hostess, had responded. Lawrence watched the spring drift of rain across the windows; he counted the flowers in the carpet. Then he reached for paper and pencil and began to scribble: "Does he paint? He fain would write a poem. . . ." Now he waited for Sarah's return.

Sarah's eyes skipped quickly down the page. The poem was light, teasing — and it was more.

> *'Tis let me see, full sixteen years*
> *And wondrous short the time appears,*
> *   Since with inquiry warm,*
> *With beauty's novel power amazed,*
> *I followed, midst the crowd, and gazed*
> *   On Siddons' beauteous form.*
>
> *Up Bath's fatiguing streets I ran,*
> *Just half-pretending to be man,*
> *   And fearful to intrude,*
>
> *   . . . .*
> *And can it be that 'neath this roof*
> *Whilst I sit patiently aloof,*
> *   This watching form can be?*
> *Quick let me fly — avaunt my fears!*
> *'Tis but a door and sixteen years*
> *   Divide this fair from me.*

Thomas Lawrence

Alas! that beauty should grow old!
Alas! that passion should grow cold!
. . . .
The devil take your doors and hours,
Your carpenters and time.

Sixteen years! She looked at him in surprise. How fast
life went! She wanted suddenly to cradle Cecilia, to comfort
Lawrence. She saw him now as he wished, no longer a
young man dreaming through an endless spring, but old
enough to want a wife or at the least, a proud, open liaison.
In Europe, she knew, it was quite customary for women in
her position to take, and openly, a younger lover. Even here,
there was Elizabeth Farren's long affair with the Earl of
Derby, and Mrs. Jordan's with the Duke of Clarence. But
no, these men were older, their positions unassailable. Either
she or Lawrence could be destroyed so easily by gossip. She
knew she loved this man, but in what way she was unsure.
Too old to be her son, he was too young — and there she
stopped.

And what of her children? She was the sole wage earner
for a family. She had long ago made her commitment, "I,
Sarah, take thee, William . . ." And she had made it again
silently, many times in the often difficult years since — a
commitment to husband and children.

Nothing more was said between them. Lawrence continued to frequent the Siddonses' house. He finished the
portrait of Sarah. And more often now, he was drawn into
the group around Sally and Maria, a group that included
one of Lawrence's younger sisters, Sarah's youngest brother

Charles Kemble, and Charles Moore and Sarah Bird. But Lawrence remained unhappy and restless.

Sarah, too, was distraught. Playing Arpasia in *Tamerlane* one night she reached the scene where Arpasia, wrought up in wild emotion, swoons to the ground. Unleashing all she felt and could express no other place than on the stage, Sarah felt her control slip. She realized too late she had crossed the fine line between acting and life. She swayed backward. The audience heard her head strike the stage, saw the awkwardness of her sprawled body. There was a moment of frightened silence, then a rush of people to the stage inquiring about her. A viewer noted, "It was long before she recovered from the fainting fit."

Then William announced that he had put ten thousand pounds of their savings into a quarter ownership of Sadler's Wells. Sarah was aghast. The Wells was a coffeehouse theatre where as a maidservant in a novel of the times wrote: "I saw such tumbling and dancing upon ropes and wires. . . . You knows as how the Witches in Wales fly upon broomsticks: but here was flying without any broomstick . . . and firing of pistols in the air, and blowing of trumpets, and swinging and rolling of wheel-barrows upon a wire." And, Sarah feared, here also was the probable loss of much of her savings. She wished William luck and quickly agreed to do more than forty performances for Sheridan that season.

Many people thought it was Sarah who had bought into Sadler's Wells and were shocked at the idea. Her image was so thoroughly set in public as the respectable housewife and great actress that one lady of fashion remarked, "Mrs. Siddons and Sadler's Wells seem to me as ill-fitted as the dish they call Toad in a Hole; which I never saw, but always think of with anger — putting a noble sirloin of beef into a poor, paltry batter pudding!"

In Marlborough Street, Maria had coaxed Tom Lawrence into doing another sketch of her and Sally. As he worked, he noted again how like her mother's face Sally's was in many ways. At twenty-one Sally had a warm dignity that attracted numerous admirers. And Lawrence was too experienced an observer of women's faces to miss what was so lately obvious in Sally's. She was in love with him. He began to respond. She was younger than he, free of commitments, and she was Sarah's daughter.

"Mother, I want to marry Tom Lawrence."

Sarah was stunned by Sally's words. With a two-year-old in the house it was hard to realize she had another child who was ready for marriage. Surely it was no more than year before yesterday she had stood in the window of 33 Paragon Street with her arm about Sally's tiny shoulders. Eighteen years ago! Sarah held out her arms and hugged her grown-up daughter close.

Yet Sarah worried — and hoped. How wonderful it would be if this marriage might work out, if these two people she loved could make a life together. But Sally's health was still poor, her asthma attacks recurrent, and her doctors gave little hope of improvement. Husbands could be impatient of illness in their wives. Sarah thought back to William's behavior, which had caused Mrs. Piozzi to remark on his "savage treatment of dear Siddons, whose present state of health demands tenderness." Would Lawrence have enough tenderness toward Sally? Could he give her the care she must have?

Perhaps time would give the answer. Lawrence was deep in debt and the sole support of his father and sisters; he could not marry immediately. Meantime, Sarah asked them to say nothing to William. He was not in the mood for young love's problems on top of those of Sadler's Wells.

Lawrence grew rebellious and angry. Now that he had decided to marry, he wanted no waiting. Then Sally became ill. And Maria offered sympathy. He was in no mood to refuse it. If Sally were not well enough to be amusing, Maria would slip quietly out of the house after her mother had left for the theatre and meet Lawrence secretly. They began to enjoy the intrigue.

As Sally recovered she soon realized what had happened between her sister and Lawrence. Like her mother, she masked the hurt under reserve, and said nothing when Lawrence formally asked permission to marry Maria. Sarah, shocked at Lawrence's swift change of heart from Sally to Maria during Sally's illness, agreed with William when he refused consent. William declared that Lawrence was unable to support a wife; the answer was no.

Maria, dashing to secret meetings with Lawrence and anxious to avoid the warm outdoor clothing which might invite questions, caught a severe cold. The cold soon developed into a lingering illness which the doctor feared would become consumption. Maria played on her parents' anxiety.

If only she could marry Lawrence she would be happy and get well. At last Sarah and William gave in. They agreed to an engagement and offered to pay all Lawrence's debts as a wedding present.

Bereft of the romantic meetings and with no family opposition to stimulate his desire, Lawrence soon found his interest in Maria waning. Her doctor insisted she must remain indoors; she expected constant attention. She was willful and vain. The better he came to know Maria, the more Lawrence appreciated Sally. Loving music, he missed the evenings when Sally had played and sung for him, often songs she had composed. Watching her steady sweetness in the face of Maria's pettish demands, he thought again how like her mother Sally was. His feeling for Maria had been a temporary excitement; Sally was the wife he wanted. But Sally now refused to listen to him.

Frantic and trapped, Lawrence appealed to Sarah. She tried to calm him, to make him realize his defection would hurt Maria, perhaps delay her recovery. He grew more hysterical in his demands. Sarah must help him! She, of all people, should understand what he felt! Sarah pleaded for patience. Lawrence stormed toward Maria's room. "I'll tell her myself! I'll tell Maria the truth!"

Sarah flung herself between Lawrence and Maria's door. "No!" She went down on her knees before him. "No. I implore you — it might kill Maria!"

In tears Lawrence ran from the house.

There was no need to tell Maria. She soon guessed from Lawrence's increasing moodiness that his feeling for her

*Sir Thomas Lawrence as an older man. Engraving
after the portrait by Charles Landseer.
(From the Raymond Mander
and Joe Mitchenson Theatre Collection)*

had changed. In February she wrote to Sarah Bird: "I agree with you that nothing can be so delightful as the *unremitting* attention of those we love, but where shall we find constancy enough in this wicked world to make us happy!"

Both Sarah and the girls had instinctively held back from discussing the situation with William. He was often at Bath taking treatment for his gouty leg, and they were wary of his increasingly harsh, negative judgments on family matters. By mid-February, Sarah knew she must talk with William. He had never known of Lawrence's first love for Sally, but outraged by his fickleness toward Maria, William ordered the young painter from the house.

Sarah was torn by guilt and indecision. Had she been wrong to ask delay in Lawrence's request to marry Sally? Or had his vacillation been just the behavior she intuitively feared? How deeply had her own feelings toward Lawrence affected her decision? Who could know? At the theatre she made a sudden and surprising move.

Sheridan was producing a new play, *The Stranger,* which he had translated from the German. Although in France freedom and equality had disappeared under the drive toward military conquest, the revolutionary ideals could never disappear. Throughout Europe ordinary people, whatever their politics, were gaining importance. They were tired of plays about ancient queens and privileged duchesses; they wanted plays about people like themselves. Mrs. Haller in *The Stranger* was such a person. Sarah went to Sheridan.

"I want to play Mrs. Haller."

Sheridan's eyebrows arched. "The respectable Mrs. Siddons play an erring wife? A woman who leaves her husband and children for a lover?"

Sarah faced him unsmiling. "I can understand her."

He asked no more questions. "Audiences will be shocked, you know. The ending is not acceptable to many people."

Sarah nodded. She knew that an unfaithful wife in eighteenth-century drama could come to only one end—death, by her own hand or her wronged husband's. *The Stranger* ended in understanding and reconciliation between the husband whose coldness had contributed to the break and his repentant wife. Their final moment was an embrace. Sarah spoke softly. "It is such a human ending."

While Sarah was studying the role, she was also nursing William through an attack of rheumatism and trying to ease Maria's bitterness which was deeper than Sally knew. Sarah saw how much the enforced idleness indoors was depressing Maria, who said in a letter: "I long so much to go out that I envy every little *beggar* running about in the open air. . . ." If *The Stranger* were successful, Sarah decided, they would give Maria a country summer.

On March 28, 1798, *The Stranger* opened. Shocked critics denounced the play. If theatres were to promote such immorality, said one, "not a child in England will have its head patted by its legitimate father." Elizabeth Inchbald referred haughtily to the "catastrophe of the conclusion." But the audience's heart was caught by the compassionate power of Sarah's acting. At last, Sheridan had a hit.

Soon after, Sally told her mother that she was writing to Lawrence and meeting him for walks in Soho Square, and that she was more in love with him than ever. Sarah was disturbed, yet she believed her daughters must make their own decisions, particularly about love. "In this *most* IMPORTANT *object of their lives*," she wrote a friend, "it has always been my system that they must decide for themselves."

Sally, sharing her delight at her mother's tacit approval of their meetings, wrote Lawrence: "my conduct is no secret to her whose approbation is as dear to me as my life." Knowing Lawrence could not afford to marry, Sally assured him: "do not suspect me of being so mad as to add to the embarrassments of him I love by giving him a wife to support." But she left him in no doubt of her love. She gave him a ring made in a Lover's Knot and wrote: "You have it, keep it, love it, nor ever part with it."

In June the Siddonses moved to Clifton for the summer. It was the place Maria had chosen, in "a very beautiful situation" overlooking woodland and a river. Sarah had wished the whole family could be together there, but the younger children's noise upset Maria, so George and Cecilia remained at their boarding schools. Sarah must, she knew, tour from July until late fall to pay the mounting family bills. Sheridan still owed her more than two thousand pounds and William's venture at Sadler's Wells was already failing.

Sarah was rapidly aware that something had changed in Sally's feeling for Lawrence. Exactly what she was unable to guess and it disturbed her that Sally did not say. They were usually very close. Sally had once said of her mother, "not only the tenderest of parents, but the sweetest and most indulgent of friends, to whom my whole heart is open, and from whose sympathy and consolation I have found comfort and happiness in moments of severe affliction." When July came Sarah suggested that Sally come along with her and William on tour. Maria was quite happy to remain in Clifton with Mrs. Pennington, an old family friend from Bath days.

The Siddonses made their headquarters in Cheltenham while Sarah played there and in nearby towns. Frequent letters from Clifton kept the family linked together. Sarah wrote often, asking for detailed news of Maria's condition; worry and gratitude to Mrs. Pennington flowed through every letter. Maria was attending balls and parties, though forbidden to dance, and seemed cheerfully convalescent. But one evening as Mrs. Pennington read aloud the story of a man who had loved two sisters, Maria broke down. She confided her love for Lawrence, her disappointment, and her fear Sally would marry him.

Early in August, Sally had a severe asthma attack. Nursing her through the difficult days and nights, Sarah listened to Sally's doubts about marrying a man so erratic and emotional as Lawrence. And at last, Sally sent a letter to him breaking off their relationship. Suddenly the news from Clifton took on an urgent note. Maria's improvement had been temporary. She was growing weaker. Sally immediately left for Clifton accompanied by the sympathetic theatre manager, Mr. Macready.

That evening Sarah's dressing-room door burst open and Lawrence stood before her demanding to see Sally, demanding to know why she had put an end to his expectations. He held out a letter. " 'A total end,' she says, 'to all intercourse between us.' "

Gently, Sarah told him "his hopes with regard to Sally . . . were entirely at an end," and that Sally had gone to be with Maria whose condition left them little hope she would ever recover. In a torrent of remorse and fury Lawrence refused to accept Sally's decision. After he left, Sarah walked slowly back to her lodgings, her heart filled with a despairing pity for her daughters and Tom Lawrence.

Next day neither Sarah nor Lawrence's sister, whom he had been visiting, could find him. Quickly Sarah sent off a letter to Mrs. Pennington warning her that Lawrence might arrive in Clifton. "I pray God," wrote Sarah, "his phrenzy may not impel him to some *desperate action!*" And she confided she had not told William any of this "as it could answer no end but to enrage *him* and make us *all* still more unhappy."

Sarah had guessed correctly. Lawrence arrived in Clifton, registered under an assumed name at a local hotel, and sent a letter to Mrs. Pennington begging her help. "Perhaps *all of my future happiness is at stake, and in your Power,*" he wrote, pleading that she give Sally the note he enclosed and warning her to silence with Maria. *"The least mention of me would be hazardous in the extreme."* He was terrified that Maria would turn Sally against him. Unable to resist tangling herself in the romance, Mrs. Pennington gave Sally his note and agreed to meet him with Sally's reply.

Sally met Lawrence, told him again to hope for nothing

from her, that she was "not a girl to be won by rant and violence."

In Birmingham several afternoons later Lawrence again burst in upon Sarah. Pleading, shouting, he paced the room "in agonies." He accused her, he accused Maria; they were setting Sally against him. He would throw away his career and exile himself to Switzerland. He would kill himself. Already near exhaustion from work and worry, Sarah twice came near fainting. Then Lawrence became all contrition. He implored her forgiveness and help. At last she was able to quiet him, and he left for London, "determined steadily to pursue a course of conduct which should regain his credit." Sarah later wrote to Mrs. Pennington: "I hope to God he *will,* for his *own* sake." Sarah was too shattered to play the evening's performance.

Sarah admitted to Mrs. Pennington that she had given way before his threats of self-destruction enough to compromise "into *toleration* of his love for Sally." Yet Sarah urged sympathy toward him. "A duteous son, a tender Brother, a kind and zealous friend; all these he is," she wrote. "Oh! That caprice and passion shou'd thus obscure the many excellencies and lofty genius of this man!"

More than anything else now Sarah relied on Sally's own steady good sense and affection. "I have receiv'd my beloved Sally's comfortable letter. "Oh, tell her how proud her *Mother is of such a child,"* Sarah wrote Mrs. Pennington.

News from Clifton became more ominous. Sally was ill with asthma and Maria's condition had changed from gradual to swift decline. William's leg was worse and he was now on crutches. Sarah hurried back to Clifton. Lawrence, meanwhile, had been bombarding Mrs. Pennington with letters urging her to plead his cause with Sally. *"Think that you are working out the happiness of two Beings destin'd (yes, with all my frailties), destined for each other by Love and Mind."*

For a short time, Maria improved under her mother's care, then she grew worse. During the night of Friday, October 5, while Sally and Mrs. Pennington sat with Maria to give Sarah some rest, Maria asked quietly if she were dying. After a moment Sally nodded. Maria lay back, apparently relieved. She spoke of her faith in God, her regret for the things she had done wrong. Then she beckoned Sally close to her. "Promise me, my Sally, *never* to be the wife of Mr. Lawrence. I *cannot* BEAR to *think* of *your* being so."

Sally evaded the promise. "Dear Maria, think of nothing that agitates you at this time." Maria persisted. "Oh, it is impossible!" Sally protested.

Maria seemed satisfied. "I am content . . ." she whispered.

Later on Saturday, sensing that her death was near, Maria began talking to her mother of when it would come and how. She asked Sarah to read her some prayers. Softly and clearly, Sarah read, " '. . . in thy mercy grant us a safe lodging, and a holy rest, and peace at the last.' " Suddenly Maria spoke of Lawrence. "Sally has promised never to marry him," Maria whispered.

In tears Sally protested, "I did *not* promise, dear, dying Angel; but I WILL and DO, if you require it."

Maria's eyes closed. "Thank you, Sally." Then, as if Lawrence's fears had dictated the scene, Maria seemed to gain strength. Rising up, she commanded, "Sally, give me your hand." As Sally did so, Maria's voice rose. "You promise never to be his wife. Mother — Mrs. Pennington — lay your hands on hers." Speechless, almost hypnotized under the force of the dying girl's determination, Sarah and Mrs. Pennington laid their hands over Sally's. "You understand? Bear witness." Releasing their hands, Maria pointed her finger at Sally. "Sally, sacred, sacred, be this promise! REMEMBER ME, and God bless you."

Maria sank back at rest. The pallor of her face disappeared in a light flush of color. Saying affectionate farewells to her family, she slipped into unconsciousness. At two o'clock on Sunday morning, the death she had said she welcomed came to Maria. She was nineteen years old.

Maria was buried in Clifton October 10, 1798. Exhausted and grief-torn, Sarah left immediately for Bath with William. There, with the Whalleys, they could find a brief rest and the comfort of understanding friends.

Back in London by mid-October, Sarah returned to work. She chose Isabella in *Measure for Measure,* a role more intellectual than emotional. Although Sarah had once said, "It is sometimes a great relief . . . that I can at least upon the stage give a full vent to the heart which . . . swells with its weight almost to bursting," this time she dared not risk it. The wound was too deep and too fresh, though the work itself was healing.

Shortly after her first performance, Sarah opened a letter from Mrs. Pennington. She had written to Lawrence, Mrs. Pennington said, and given him the details of Maria's death and Sally's oath. He had responded with a note she enclosed. Sarah read the note in growing horror. Lawrence's handwriting wavered and plunged. He had underlined some words in strokes nearly a quarter of an inch thick. The news of Sally's promise to Maria had obviously sent him close to the brink of madness:

> It is only my hand that shakes, not my mind.
>
> I have played deeply for her, and you think she will still escape me. I'll tell you a Secret. *It is possible she may.* MARK THE END. . . .

Chapter Fourteen

Aftermath

IMMEDIATELY upon reading Lawrence's wild note, Sarah went to the Twisses. Yes, said her sister and brother-in-law, Lawrence was frequently at their home; he had been dreadfully upset but was now more composed. He was still determined to marry Sally. Though Frances was somewhat distressed by Lawrence's emotional outbursts, she and her husband both spoke their disapproval of the oath Maria had demanded of Sally. An extorted promise, they said, counted for nothing.

For Sally, the oath stood rocklike between her and Tom Lawrence. And she confided to her mother, she was more and more repelled by his emotional violence. "If this is love, defend me from it." Admittedly, Sally chafed under the promise, yet she clung to it, saying, "Whatever I may *feel* I will *act* AS I HAVE PROMISED."

Watching her gentle, music-loving daughter, Sarah wondered if perhaps Sally needed this defense against the stormy love she lacked the vigor to match. Whatever her own daydreams had once been of cradling and playing with grandchildren who were the sons and daughters of Lawrence and Sally, Sarah now said, "I am more and more convinced they would both be wretched."

Gossip within the family was spreading outward. Sarah acknowledged that she must stop evading a discussion with William. When Mrs. Pennington had first urged it, Sarah had responded that William was, "unhappily, so cold and repelling, that instead of tender sympathy I should expect harsh words." Now as she feared, William received the story of Sally's tangled love with "coldness and reserve," the reaction which Sarah wrote "has always check'd my tongue and chilled my heart in every occurrence of importance *thro' our lives.*" Then defending him, she added, "No, it is not his *fault,* it is his *nature.*" When Sarah pleaded with him to give Sally the fatherly understanding she needed, William faced his daughter and "testified his total disapprobation, nay abhorrence" of her having anything whatever to do with Lawrence.

After this scene Sarah nursed Sally through the ensuing asthma attacks and continued to worry about both her and Lawrence. Of her daughter she wrote: "Our poor dear Sally has had a sad winter of it." And of Lawrence: "There is a corner yet left in my heart that feels for this unhappy creature, and still yearns toward him, when I think of the happy hours we have all spent together under this roof."

She cautioned Mrs. Pennington, who was furious with him, to have "compassion on his reputation."

Sally made her own decision. She wrote that the Lawrence she loved had existed only in her imagination and that "time and circumstance have discovered to me a character which nothing could tempt me to unite myself to." When Lawrence wrote her a pleading letter, Sally answered "in so decisive a manner . . . as to extinguish in a short time all hope."

During this time the troubles at Drury Lane continued. William fumed and fussed, trying to decide whether Sarah should return there or not. His final decision was yes, it was the only way she could hope to collect any of her back salary. Sheridan was producing another translation from the German, a play called *Pizarro*. He wanted Sarah to play Elvira, Pizarro's mistress. The play had political overtones; Pizarro, general of the Spanish conquerors of Peru is opposed by the heroic Peruvian, Rolla. England, with her first major victory over Napoleon's conquering armies, was ready, Sheridan thought, for such a play. He scored his adaptation with the same brilliant political writing that had characterized his greatest Parliamentary speeches.

In an echo of Macbeth, he disagreed with Sarah over her playing Elvira. "I tell you," insisted Sheridan, "this woman is a common camp follower."

"No! She has a strong, savage nobility."

When *Pizarro* opened on May 24, 1799, Sarah again proved to be right. John Philip, amused at his sister's stubborn triumph, remarked, "My sister made a heroine of a soldier's trull." So accurately had Sheridan taken England's political pulse, however, that after the play closed the Marquis of Queensberry asked why stocks had tumbled. "Because," said his broker, "at Drury Lane they have left off acting *Pizarro*."

That summer, as usual, Sarah went on tour. One afternoon, at an inn where she was staying, she noticed a little girl staring at her. Sarah smiled and spoke to the child. Years later when she was grown, the child still remembered how fascinated she had been by the long lashes and beautiful eyes of the actress, and how, encouraged by Sarah's smile she had said softly, "Mama says you are the great Mrs. Siddons." Then, blinking fast against tears, "I shall never be able to see you act! I have to go away to the country tonight."

Responsive as always to children, Sarah dried the little girl's tears. "Never mind. I shall act for you now if you like." And there in the common room of the inn, Sarah played a dramatic bit from Milton and two of her famous scenes from Shakespeare for an enraptured audience of one.

At the beginning of the fall season of 1800, John Philip again became manager of Drury Lane. He and Sarah were hopeful it could be made profitable and that they might become part owners. Feeling that they were moving toward the peak of their careers, they wanted more control over their work, the fitting climax of playing in their own theatre. Sheridan was enthusiastic. He pledged greater financial stability. Within weeks, however, John Philip was writing desperate notes to the theatre treasurer, begging for money for paint, costume material, payment for the actors.

The season was a depressing one at Drury Lane. One after another, new plays failed, including one by Mr. Whalley that not even Sarah's acting could redeem from the irritable yawns of the audience. When she played in a new tragedy, *de Montfort,* John outdid himself providing impressive Gothic stage sets. But as the play sank into a swamp of gloom, the only cheer the critics could offer was that "Mrs. Siddons did her utmost with the Countess Jane," and "Mr. Kemble provided a very unusual pile of scenery."

Sally's health was a constant worry to Sarah, but six-year-old Cecilia was proving a merry-hearted addition to the family. "Witty and pretty," Sarah described her. After Cecilia was taken to see *Bluebeard* she kept the household entertained for weeks. Climbing on chairs and tables, "she has done nothing but act Sister Anne upon the tower, waving her handkerchief ever since," wrote Sally.

While her youngest was playing Sister Anne upon the tower, Sarah's eldest, Henry, was scheduled to play Hamlet at Covent Garden. She was in a fret of motherly concern, writing to Elizabeth Inchbald: "I was frightened when I yesterday received information of it. Oh, I hope to God he will get through it." After Henry had given a less than brilliant performance, Sarah wrote loyally: "My son Henry's success has been a very great comfort to me. I do think, if I can divest myself of partiality, that it was a very respectable first attempt."

In spite of the strain of grief and worry, critics noted that in this, her forty-sixth year, Sarah was as beautiful, if not more beautiful than she had ever been. Mrs. Piozzi, with a friend's keen eye noted that, after a brief illness, Sarah was "thin as a lath, and light as air." And Sarah was once again seeing Thomas Lawrence. He had written a formal note asking to be received. Sally appeared pleased, immediately writing to a friend: "I am glad my mother has seen Mr. Lawrence, I mean talk'd with him."

There had been chance meetings with Lawrence at the theatre and at church, and Sally had pointedly ignored him. Now she soon began resenting the friendly attitude her family — except for her father — adopted toward Lawrence. To Sarah Bird, she confided: "You may have heard (and it is true) of Mr. L. being in Mrs. Kemble's box, and with my mother. He is frequently at my Uncle's house, and I believe scarcely ever misses a night when my mother performs, when he generally pays her a visit in her dressing room. This I hear not from my mother, for unless I force her to it, she never mentions him." Sarah had noticed that after meetings with Lawrence, however brief, Sally's asthma had worsened. She continued to speak little of her own meetings with Lawrence, unaware that Sally was complaining to Sarah Bird:

> I know my mother sees him often, and I know she cannot cease to look on him with the partiality she always did, and always will, I believe feel for him, yet she never mentions him to me, never tells me he has spoken of me, or desires to be remembered to me — perhaps indeed he never *does* think

or speak of me. . . . However *right* I may think it we are separated, I would not have him *forget me!*

Sally began attempting to attract Lawrence's attention at the theatre. When he ignored her she asked Sarah Bird to "ask him *from me* what I have done." The result was a letter from Lawrence as definite as Sally's had been to him when he appealed to her after Maria's death.

Sarah, noting the increased feverishness of Sally's condition, was furious with Sarah Bird for acting as romantic go-between. Wearily, she probed her heart for a way to explain to this beloved daughter her own continuing protective friendship for Thomas Lawrence.

In the spring of 1802 Sarah began work on a role she had long wanted to do, Hermione in *The Winter's Tale.* It was nearly her last role. As she stood posed in the statue scene one evening, she smelled an odor of burning cloth. Dear God, not fire backstage! She went rigid until the scene finished. Turning, she saw the train of her gown had been burned off where it lay draped behind her. A scene shifter had noticed the fold of material blow across a nearby lamp and instantly going on his knees had crawled forward to smother the flame. Sarah knew he had saved her from death or terrible burns. "Surrounded as I was with muslin, the flame would have run like wildfire," she wrote.

Soon after, the man's son, in a moment of despair, deserted from the army. He had been caught and was due to be flogged. Immediately Sarah bombarded her influential friends, begging them to help the boy. She dashed to their homes at breakfast or dinner if need be. For days all her spare time was taken up in writing letters to those she could not meet, trying to get the boy "saved from the disgrace and hideous torture of the lash to which he has exposed himself. I hope to God I shall succeed." Thankfully, the man told Sarah later that she had indeed succeeded.

By the season's end in June, 1802, Sarah and John Philip were meeting in tense, troubled conferences. Sheridan's careless ways were reaching an impossible point. Sarah and John were unable to do good work. They were constantly upset. Yet their old friendship for Sheridan made any decision deeply difficult. At last they decided to accept Covent Garden's offer to move there. John could buy into the management and both would receive excellent terms in addition to greater peace. Their engagement would begin in the fall of 1803 and meanwhile John would take the year off and travel in Europe, leaving contract negotiations to their old friend, Elizabeth Inchbald.

Sarah wished she could join her brother on the holiday. The years of strain, grief, and work were taking their toll. She had suffered a painful infection, erysipelas, inside her lips, and her doctor warned it might recur. She began having the age-old actor's nightmare of losing her teeth. "I dreamed all my teeth fell out on the stage," she admitted.

Her dentist clucked sympathetically. Such was the progress being made, he informed her, they could now place a lining in cavities before filling them to prevent further decay. To Sarah's question of what this miracle substance might be, he replied, "Why, it is — ah — sparrows' droppings. The lime, you know." At her horrified expression, he added, "It does save the teeth, dear lady!"

For Sarah there was no choice but work until she and John should start at Covent Garden. William had lost almost all the ten thousand pounds he had invested in Sadler's Wells; he and Sally both required constant medical care, and the cost of living rose as the war continued. She wrote Mrs. Piozzi that she was going on tour to Ireland and though happy she could provide for her family, "I hope it is not wrong to say, I am tired, and should be glad to be at rest indeed."

Sally was now well enough to enjoy parties and the company of Charles Moore who was in love with her. Sarah would take Patty Wilkinson, Tate's daughter, with her to Ireland as companion. All seemed satisfactorily arranged, yet as the time neared for her departure, Sarah was filled with restless foreboding. She visited her parents, and left, certain she would never see her father again. Almost in panic, she wrote Mrs. Piozzi: "I commit my children to your friendly protection, with a full and perfect reliance on the goodness you have always manifested."

Hoping to return to England by Christmas, Sarah finished her fall season only to be met with William's insistence she remain in Ireland and earn additional money. He was having the house in Great Marlborough Street redecorated, and their son, George, needed expensive outfitting for his new position in the East India Company. Sarah stayed, a desperately lonely woman living on letters from home.

In one, Sally told of Henry's wedding. And Sarah laughed and cried through the description of her son's stage fright, how his knees shook so badly he had to clutch the altar rail for support and cried out, "I will!" before the minister asked the question.

George spent two weeks with Sarah before leaving for India. Knowing he meant to stay there permanently, Sarah found the visit a bittersweet joy that left her lonelier than before. In December came news of her father's death. Sarah turned to the proffered friendship of a young couple in the company, Mr. and Mrs. Galindo. She accepted their suggestion that having no carriage of her own, she let Mr. Galindo drive her about in their curricle. Impulsively pouring out her need to give and to love, Sarah loaned them money and offered her help in finding them work at Covent Garden. She failed to suspect they might be using her for their own gain.

Early in March, as Sarah was getting ready to leave for Cork, in the south of Ireland, Patty Wilkinson had a letter from William. Sally was very ill, he said, but Patty was not to tell Sarah. Alarmed, Patty gave the letter to Sarah. Immediately, Sarah tried to get passage for England. No ships were leaving, she was told. Gales were raging across the Irish Sea. No ships of any kind could put to sea. Frantic, Sarah paced the storm-ridden waterfront docks and prayed.

Two days later, another letter arrived from William. Sally was better, he assured them. There was no reason to worry, no reason for Sarah to return. She must play her engagement in Cork. Obediently, Sarah went to Cork, but she wrote Mrs. Fitzhugh, who was helping to care for Sally: "Would to God I were at her bedside! . . . The suspense that distance keeps me in you may imagine, but it cannot be described."

Violent storms battered the Irish coast continually. Letters were delayed. Sarah determined to get back to Sally no matter what anyone wrote. She talked to the theatre manager, who at once released her from her contract. But the answer from the shipping offices was still no. There were no ships leaving the harbor. With Patty, Sarah took a stagecoach along the drenched, windy roads back to Dublin. Perhaps she might find some kind of boat sailing from there. Still no ships were putting to sea. At last, Sarah secured passage to Holyhead, Wales.

From Holyhead, Sarah and Patty went on immediately by post chaise. When they arrived at Shrewsbury in northern England, a letter from William awaited them. It had been written several days before; it warned Sarah to expect the worst. Sally was near death. As Sarah read the letter, Patty was called from the room. She returned, pale and stricken. Sarah knew without being told. Her beloved Sally was dead.

For long moments Sarah stood without moving. Then she lay down on her bed, as Patty said later, "in speechless despondency." She remained there, for more than a day, "cold and torpid as a stone." Sarah's brother Charles hurried to meet her and took her to their mother's home. Later in the summer she went to a farm near Cheltenham with Cecilia and Patty, a place away from watching eyes. The rest of the summer was spent "reading under a haystack" and "musing in the orchard," where there were "no observers near to say I am mad, foolish, or melancholy." Sarah would like to have stayed longer, but John Philip was urging her to London. They must begin their work at Covent Garden.

In September, John Philip played his first performance at Covent Garden, which he now owned a sixth part of, as Macbeth. Three nights later, Sarah followed as Isabella in *The Fatal Marriage*. As the season continued, critics and audience noted that personal tragedy had deepened the passionate intensity of Sarah's acting. Now her Lady Macbeth was rent with her own sorrow, torn by Sarah's own self-questioning. One critic wrote: "None knew the troubled grandeur of guilt till they saw her in Lady Macbeth . . . more hideously haunted than ever was the hollow grave, seemed then, to be the cell of her heart."

By March of 1804 Lawrence was again painting Sarah's portrait. Commissioned by Mrs. Fitzhugh, the painting was of Sarah giving a reading at Court. It would be perhaps the ugliest — and most truthful — Lawrence ever painted of a woman. In the darkly tragic face of his sitter, in the violent brush strokes of red and black, were all the fury and tragedy of their own impossible love. Lawrence's heart and brush raged against the changes he saw time and grief making in the woman before him.

The sessions in his studio were long, broken by talk of many things. Sarah was still depressed, Lawrence still torn by his love for Sally, and for Sarah herself. Together, Sarah

*William Siddons as an older man. Engraving
from the portrait by John Opie.
(The Tate Gallery, London)*

and Thomas Lawrence could work out their guilt and grief in unguarded talk, in the freedom of their more than twenty-year friendship. Yet now, when they fully understood each other's hearts, the shadows of the dead lay between them.

Gossip soon went round London that Mrs. Siddons was sitting by candlelight to Thomas Lawrence until two in the morning. William had retired permanently to Bath, the only place where his health was at all improved. Rumors flew that the Siddonses were seeking a divorce, that Sarah and Thomas Lawrence were lovers, that they had eloped together. At last, in November, William placed a notice in the papers offering a thousand pounds' reward for information leading to the perpetrator of these "most wicked and injurious slanders." No more was heard of the matter. William returned to Bath and Sarah began to dismantle the house in Great Marlborough Street.

When everything had been packed and sent to storage or to the new lodgings Sarah had taken for herself and Cecilia in Hanover Square, Sarah made a final check through the empty house: her upstairs sitting room, Maria's room, Sally's. Opening a window, she looked out on the rain-burnished roofs of neighboring houses, watched the smoke drifting and rising from the chimney pots as Sally had so often done, loving the city after her return from school. Suddenly, Sarah bent over, gripping the window ledge until pain shot through her arms. Sally — dear shy Sally . . . beautiful, vain Maria . . . noisy little George. . . . Why must it all be over? All the laughter and hope and music, the rollicking shouts of small boys and tiny, sudsy arms reaching to be lifted from the huge iron bathtub. I want it back! Oh God, I want it back! The silent cry tore through her.

An hour later she was in her dressing room at Covent Garden.

Pouring her own heart's sorrow into her work, Sarah now achieved a position of "undisputed supremacy" but she played no new roles, experimented with no new plays. The great creative drive was over; those she had loved were dead or parted from her. Without their love, she had little reason for the adventure of creating.

In January 1808, Sarah spent a month in Bath with William. Though they no longer maintained a home together, there remained affection and memory between them. William had not been well, and Sarah wanted to be with him. When he appeared recovered, Sarah returned to London. On March 11, she received word of William's sudden death. Five days later, Sarah knelt in Bath Abbey as the prayers of the burial service were said for William. He had been sixty-seven years old. But Sarah remembered the young man, her Sid, on a morning long ago when they had stood together under this same vaulted ceiling as Maria was christened. Now there was no one to remember that moment with her.

Chapter Fifteen

Fire and Fury

IT WAS NEARLY MIDNIGHT on September 19, 1808, when Sarah left the theatre. She had stayed late after a performance of *Pizarro,* talking to friends, then sorting through some costumes and properties she had moved to the theatre after leaving Great Marlborough Street. Feeling the oddly haunting quiet of an empty theatre settle around her, she bade the watchman goodnight and went home. The watchman decided to have a nap before going on his rounds.

Four hours later he was startled out of a comfortable sleep by frantic pounding on his door. "Fire! Fire!" Guiltily he fumbled for his keys. The stage door near his office crashed open. Men were running in all directions. He was being dragged out by William Addicott, the stage carpenter. "The theatre's on fire!" yelled Addicott.

On the street, firemen were struggling to attach hoses to the square, wooden-boxed pumping engines. Covent Garden was aflame from roof to cellar. Addicott and others beat on the doors where the theatre's own fire equipment was kept. No one could find keys. Smashing their way in, they hauled the engine out only to find the hoses were too short. Within minutes, everyone in the neighborhood was running about with wet cloths, picking up flaming splinters, trying to keep the fire from spreading. But wind caught the flames, spun them along rooftops and in through open windows. On the Hart Street side of the theatre four houses directly across the street burst into flames at the same moment. Someone shouted that Drury Lane, only a short distance away, might catch at any moment from the wind-driven fire flakes. People scrambled to the roof, mounting guard, ready to open Drury's rooftop reservoirs of water.

The Phoenix Fire Engine arrived; the firemen pulled and shoved until they maneuvered it through the great door on Covent Garden Piazza, where they could play the hoses on the interior of the theatre. Addicott made his way to the chief fireman. "Great God, man, you're right under the scene shop! It's already blazing! Get out! Get back out!"

"Mind your own business!" yelled the firemen. Addicott no more than gained the outside when there was a series of thundering explosions, like a train of gunpowder going off someone said later. The scene shop and upper floors collapsed burying the Phoenix firemen under tons of fiery debris.

When John Philip ran to the scene at six o'clock in the morning, his theatre was a burning rubbish heap. Dead and dying were being carried from the ruins. Surrounding houses lay in smoldering wreckage. The Smugglers Tavern was gone, as was part of the Shakespeare Tavern with its relics of English theatre. No one knew how many dead or injured might be under the still-burning timbers of Covent Garden.

Cecilia ran into her mother's room with the news. Dressing in frantic haste Sarah rushed to the Kembles' house. John Philip's wife sat on the sofa, tears coursing down her face. Sarah's brother, Charles, huddled on a chair, his cloak reeking of smoke and ash. John, in a state of wild shock, stood before his shaving glass and stared into it blankly. From time to time he drew a razor across his face, not really noticing whether he shaved or not. Unable to speak of the lives lost, he occasionally jerked out a word or phrase, cataloguing the irreplaceable treasures lost: the magnificent pipe organ Handel built, the collection of original music manuscripts, the library of play manuscripts dating from Shakespeare's day. "God be praised," Sarah wrote to friends, "that the fire did not break out while the people were in the house!!!"

Later, staring at the wreckage, Sarah could see only what the London *Times* next day listed as "a few pieces of painted trumpery lying on the pavement," the banners of the Spanish and Peruvian processions which "had amused the town with mimic show" only a few hours before. And in the ruins, she knew, were the mutilated remains of men. This ends it all, she thought, I will never act again.

She had lost all the costumes, jewels, laces she had collected over thirty years, some of great value, some which she loved as souvenirs of her great moments on the stage. But her main thought was for John Philip. She wrote: "My poor brother has to begin the world again."

Offers of help came quickly. Money was subscribed to build a new Covent Garden, and in December of 1808, the Prince of Wales laid the cornerstone of the new theatre in a rain-soaked ceremony that left them all chilled and sneezing. Sarah, who had hoped for her lucky omen of sunshine, watched the black plumes of her hat droop soggily and fought off a presentiment of trouble.

Before the new Covent Garden opened, London would see more fires of equally suspicious origin, most of them in government buildings or those which, like the theatre, held a Royal Patent. The theatre in Manchester went, the east wing of St. James's Palace where the King and Queen lived, the New Sessions House, Westminster. Rumors flew that a train of gunpowder had been found planted in the King's Theatre.

London grew panicky. Coincidence had been strained too far. Incendiaries must be at work, said everyone. There had been too much talk lately of the republican ideas from France — not the ideals of freedom and brotherhood of the gentle, thoughtful men of early revolutionary times, but the demands of those who advocated violence and destruction.

Five months after Covent Garden burned, a messenger rushed into a late session of Parliament. He ran to Sheridan. "The Theatre Royal in Drury Lane, sir!" A motion was offered to adjourn that the members might go with Sheridan to offer what help they could. He thanked them and declined. Let the work of government go on; his troubles were his own. A short time later he stood before the flaming shell of Drury Lane. It was too late to do anything. It had been too late from the beginning. As with Covent Garden, the flames had seemed to spring out from all over the theatre at once; explosions were heard, though the theatre kept only a small amount of gunpowder on hand for stage use. Friends found Sheridan sitting in the Piazza Coffee House across the street from Drury Lane, a decanter of wine before him. "Cannot a man take a glass of wine before his own fireside?" he smiled. The brilliant, bedeviled theatre career of Richard Brinsley Sheridan was over.

Sarah, heartsick at the sight of Drury's ruins, questioned her world and the way it turned. Was this the culmination of that dawn of freedom they had hailed? She thought of the young firemen crushed in the wreckage of Covent Garden, the young shopkeeper trying to help and dying from exhaustion. Her old distrust of mindless, violent action returned in a surge of anger. But she was unprepared for the riotous opening of Covent Garden.

New Covent Garden was, agreed everyone, the most beautiful of London theatres. The colors were soft pink and dove gray, the pillars and decoration gold, the doors opening into the private boxes polished mahogany. A new row of private boxes had been built opening into a salon where the patrons could chat with friends between acts. Crystal chandeliers holding wax candles lit the house. Three hundred of the new patent gas lights illumined the stage. And to pay for all this elegance, ticket prices had been raised.

For the opening night, September 18, 1809, Sarah and John Philip would star in *Macbeth*. Sarah's costume, modeled after the wedding dress of Mary, Queen of Scots, blazed with diamonds. John had seen to the building of wonderfully accurate scenery. Yet there was an air of foreboding about the venture.

The audience had a curious preponderance of men. They were restive before the curtain rose. As John Philip stepped forward to make the opening address, the theatre shrieked with catcalls, whistles, boos and hisses. Rattles, trumpets, posthorns appeared from under coats and were added to the din.

Backstage, the frightened actors faced John Philip. They would play the show, said John. An image of black plumes in the rain crossed Sarah's mind. As the play began, the noise from the house overpowered the attempts of the actors to make themselves heard. Insulting and obscene placards were pulled out and draped over the gallery railings. The shouts became a rhythmic chant, "Old Prices! Old Prices!" People in the pit began dancing in the aisles to the beat of the chant. *Macbeth* continued, probably, said one paper, as the finest pantomime ever seen on the London stage. Only the resonant scorn of Sarah's voice could occasionally be heard.

Suddenly a lighted candle was tossed onto the stage. Terrified, the managers called the Bow Street police. Three of them arrived quickly and read the Riot Act. At last the theatre was cleared. The next night the O.P. Riots resumed. The rioters, enraged that John Philip did not come forward to address them regarding their demands, began to yell, "Onto the stage! Get onto the stage!" A technician threw the trapdoors in the stage floor open, blocking the rioters, and, said the London *Times:* "the managers had now recourse to instruments of terror, letting loose a posse of Bow Street officers from the stage doors." The theatre was again cleared by the constables, and the outraged *Times* wrote: "they took into custody several persons, who were only exercising the freedom of Englishmen, in speaking their opinions in a public Theatre."

Furious charges hit the papers. The Kemble-Siddons clan was making enormous profits out of the pockets of their audiences! For a few nights the theatre was closed while a government-appointed committee looked into the affairs of Covent Garden. The committee, including the Governor of the Bank of England, assured the public that at best the managers were making a slender profit. Stage jewels, after all, were not real diamonds. Public fury was not assuaged. Sarah and John Philip had built an enviable position; for the second time in her life, envy lashed out destructively.

The government, in fear now of a war-tired, restive people, did nothing further. John's carriage was set upon, the windows smashed. His family lived with escape ladders at the back windows in case of attack. Sarah, her fear of mobs now turned to scorn, refused to return to the theatre. The Old Price Riots went on for more than sixty nights as the actors went through their unheard lines onstage. It became fashionable to attend the riots and not the play. Eventually, John and the other owners of Covent Garden gave in and reduced the price of tickets. The rioting died out. Yet Sarah delayed her return to Covent Garden.

There was a new reason why she now held back, reluctant to expose herself to public view. Catherine Galindo had this year published a booklet of letters Sarah had written to her and Mr. Galindo in the years of their friendship. The booklet also contained Mrs. Galindo's accusation that Sarah had, with "satanic barbarity," wrecked the Galindos' marriage and alienated Mr. Galindo's affections.

The friendship had been an unfortunate one. When John and his co-managers had refused to hire the Galindos at Covent Garden, Sarah had helped them with money and influence to find other work. Their desire to use her had gradually become clear, and Sarah had finally refused to help them any more. Now Mrs. Galindo put before the public the foolishly revealing, affectionate letters Sarah had written out of loneliness and grief.

The Kemble family were enraged. They urged Sarah to sue the woman. She refused, and wrote to her nephew, Horace Twiss:

What would be the result . . . Damages or Imprisonment, I should suppose, and the failure of the first what should I gain by the second? There are three children, all under nine years old too, that must be reduced in either case to a state of wretchedness and perhaps absolute want of bread. . . .

Summing up the year, Sarah wrote: "What a time it has been with us all; beginning with fire and continuing with fury!" She was thinking now of summing up, of endings.

In April, Sarah returned to Covent Garden. She could still pack the house. Young men still adored her and wrote poetry in her praise. But she was growing stout and very tired. At one performance her ample hips failed to clear the arms of her chair — and the chair rose with her. Thomas Lawrence, still attending most of her plays, winced to hear her voice break "from want of strength" at the end of a powerful speech.

Sarah had often wanted rest; she had always enjoyed the few holidays she had taken. Now she knew that to quit the stage entirely would be for her, as it had been for David Garrick, a foretaste of death. She understood the truth of her characters' hearts and minds more deeply than ever before. But she faced herself in the mirror and knew her body could no longer fully express that truth. "I was an honest actress," she whispered.

She announced her intended retirement. It was 1812 and Sarah was fifty-seven. As Garrick had, Sarah once more played each of her great roles. On the night of June 22, she played her final performance — Lady Macbeth. The theatre was packed to the roof. At the end of the sleepwalking scene, the audience rose, shouting for the curtain to come down. They cared nothing for the rest of the play. They wanted no anticlimax.

Minutes later, the curtain rose again. Sarah, in a simply cut white dress, sat before a table. A tumult of applause greeted her — that sound familiar for over forty years. She looked out into the house remembering a candlelit barn at the King's Head Inn, the "desperate tranquillity" of her second London debut, the night she played Lady Macbeth in Sir Joshua's black and crimson costume. Now it was over.

She rose and came forward, seeing the tears on nearby faces looking up at her from the pit. She curtsied deeply. As Sarah began to speak the words of her farewell address, a profound silence filled the great house. Her voice was clear and steady:

> *Who has not felt how growing use endears*
> *The fond remembrance of our former years?*
> *Who has not sigh'd, when doom'd to leave at last*
> *The hopes of youth, the habits of the past,*
>
> . . . .
>
> *Yes! At this moment crowd my mind*
> *Scenes of bright days forever left behind,*
> *Bewildering visions of enraptur'd youth*
> *When hope and fancy wore the hues of truth,*
>
> . . . .
>
> *Perhaps your hearts, when years have glided by*
> *And past emotions wake a fleeting sigh,*
> *May think on her whose lips have pour'd so long*
> *The charmed sorrows of your Shakespeare's song:*

On her, who parting to return no more,
Is now the mourner she but seemed before:
Herself subdu'd resigns the melting spell,
And breathes, with swelling heart, her long,
Her last farewell.

The audience, some of whom remembered her as a slim young mother, beautiful and lithe, rose to their feet weeping and cheering. They saw John Philip appear beside her, take her arm and walk with her, as tears streaming down her face, she made her exit into the quiet years ahead when she would remember in the late afternoon dusk, "This is the time I would be leaving for the theatre. . . ."

Epilogue

SARAH RETIRED to Westbourne Farm with Cecilia, where she worked at her sculpture, gave parties, and enjoyed the country life. In 1817 she moved back into London and took a house at number 27 Upper Baker Street. Here, as at Westbourne, she built a studio for her modeling. In 1813 Sarah took Cecilia and Patty Wilkinson with her on a trip to France.

There were several attempts to persuade her to return to the stage, but she refused, except for a few benefit performances for members of her family. She did continue to give readings of Shakespeare and Milton to enthusiastic private audiences. Sarah and Thomas Lawrence continued to correspond from time to time, though neither made any attempt to resume their former close friendship. When Sarah was in her seventies, she said once to her youngest brother, Charles, "When I die, I wish to be carried to my grave by you and Lawrence." When Lawrence heard this, "he threw down his pencil . . . and, with his eyes full of tears and face convulsed, exclaimed, 'Good God, did she say that?' " But Thomas Lawrence died seventeen months before Sarah did.

On June 8, 1831, at the age of seventy-six, Sarah died from a recurrence of the old erysipelas infection. Five thousand people attended her funeral at Paddington Church, including the combined companies of Covent Garden and Drury Lane. In silence they bade farewell to the actress of whom it was said, "for her *to be*, was to be sublime!"

Sources Consulted

ARESTY, ESTHER B. *The Delectable Past*. New York: Simon & Schuster, 1964.

BOADEN, JAMES. *Memoirs of Mrs. Siddons*. London: Gibbings, 1893. 1 vol. ed.

BOSWELL, JAMES. *The Life of Samuel Johnson*. New York: Random House. Modern Library ed., n.d.

BRONOWSKI, J., and MALISH, BRUCE. *The Western Intellectual Tradition*. New York: Harper, 1960.

CHURCHILL, WINSTON S. *The Age of Revolution*. New York: Dodd, Mead, 1966.

DAVENPORT, MILLIA. *The Book of Costume*. New York: Crown, 1948. 1 vol. ed.

FITZGERALD, PERCY. *The Kembles*. 2 vols. London: Tinsley Brothers, 1871.

DICKENS, CHARLES. *Barnaby Rudge*. London, New York, Toronto: Oxford University Press, 1954.

FREEDLY, GEORGE, and REEVES, JOHN A. *A History of the Theatre*. New York: Crown, 1941.

FRIEDELL, EGON. *A Cultural History of the Modern Age*. Vol. 2. New York: Knopf, 1954.

GIBBS, LEWIS. *Sheridan, His Life and His Theatre*. London: Dent, 1948.

JERROLD, CLARE. *The Story of Dorothy Jordan*. London: Eveleigh Nash, 1914.

237

Sources

KENNARD, NINA A. *Mrs. Siddons.* Boston: Roberts Brothers, 1887.
MACKENZIE, KATHLEEN. *The Great Sarah.* London: Evans, 1968.
MACMILLAN, DOUGALD. *Drury Lane Calendar 1747–1776.* Oxford University Press, 1938.
MANVELL, ROGER. *Sarah Siddons, Portrait of an Actress.* New York: Putnam's, 1971.
MARINACCI, BARBARA. *Leading Ladies.* New York: Dodd, Mead, 1961.
NAGLER, A. M. *A Source Book in Theatrical History.* New York: Dover, 1952.
NETTLETON, GEORGE H., and CASE, ARTHUR E., eds. *British Dramatists from Dryden to Sheridan.* Boston: Houghton Mifflin, 1939.
NICOLL, ALLARDYCE. *The Development of the Theatre.* London: Harrap, 1927.
OXFORD, LYNN. *Playing Period Plays.* London: Garnet Miller, 1957.
PARSENS, MRS. CLEMENT. *The Incomparable Siddons.* New York: Putnam's, 1909.
ROYDE-SMITH, NAOMI. *The Private Life of Mrs. Siddons: A Psychological Investigation.* London: Gollancz, 1933.
SOBEL, BERNARD, ed. *The Theatre Handbook.* New York: Crown, 1940.
STEBBINS, LUCY POATE. *London Ladies.* New York: Columbia University Press, 1952.
TREVELYAN, G. M. *English Social History.* New York, London, Toronto: Longmans, Green, 1942.

Newspapers, Periodicals and Pamphlets

The City of Bath: Official Guidebook 1960. Published by the Spa Committee of the Bath City Council.
The Times (London), September 21, 22, and 24, 1808, and September 19. 20, and 30, 1809.
The Gentleman's Magazine, September 1809.